D0916191

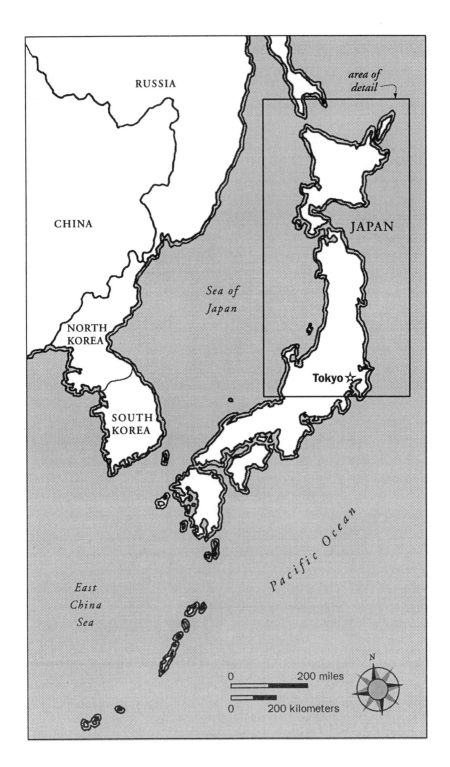

Japan

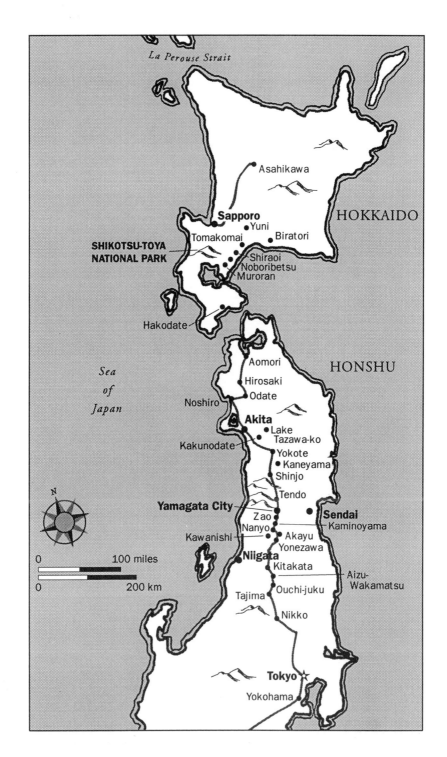

Route to the North

ADVENTURES IN JAPAN

A literary journey
in the footsteps of a Victorian lady

Evelyn Kaye

Preface by Jan Morris

Blue Panda Publications
Boulder, Colorado

Blue Panda Publications
3031 Fifth Street
Boulder, CO 80304-2501
Tel: 303 449-8474
Fax: 303 449-7525
E-mail: ekaye@ibm.net

Every effort has been made to ensure the accuracy of the information in this book, but the world of travel changes from day to day. The publisher takes no responsibility for inaccuracies relating to the travel information included. As a courtesy to the people mentioned in the book, their real names have not been used.

© Copyright 2000 by Evelyn Kaye
First Edition
Printed in the United States of America

Book Design: Christopher Sarson
Cover design: George Roche Design
Cover photos: Evelyn Kaye
Maps: Molly O'Halloran

Publisher's Cataloging-in-Publication
(Provided by Quality Books, Inc.)

Kaye, Evelyn, 1937-
   Adventures in Japan : a literary journey in the
footsteps of a Victorian lady / by Evelyn Kaye. --
1st ed.
    p. cm.
   Includes bibliographical references and index.
   LCCN: 99-80131
   ISBN: 1-929315-00-7

   1. Japan--Guidebooks. 2. Japan--History--19th
century. 3. Literary journeys--Japan.
4. Literary landmaks--Japan--Guidebooks.
I. Title.

DS805.2.K39 2000   915.204'49
                      QBI00-297

Books by Evelyn Kaye

Amazing Traveler: Isabella Bird
Free Vacations & Bargain Adventures in the USA
Active Woman Vacation Guide
American Society of Journalists and Authors 50th Anniversary Journal,
                                                                    Editor
Travel and Learn: The New Guide to Educational Travel 1994-5
Family Travel: Terrific New Ideas for Today's Families
Eco-Vacations: Enjoy Yourself and Save the Earth
College Bound with J. Gardner
The Parents Going-Away Planner with J. Gardner
The Hole In The Sheet
Write and Sell Your TV Drama! with A. Loring
Relationships in Marriage and the Family, with Stinnett and Walters
Crosscurrents: Children, Families & Religion
The Family Guide to Cape Cod with B. Chesler
How To Treat TV with TLC
The Family Guide to Childrens Television
Action for Childrens Television, Editor

The Author

Evelyn Kaye's travels began when she sailed to Canada from England as a child with her grandmother and ended up living in Toronto for almost four years. She's traveled ever since. After school in England, she lived for a year in France and in Israel. She's toured Italy, Sicily, Denmark, Sweden, Belgium, the Netherlands, Switzerland, Mexico, Ecuador, Australia, New Zealand, and India. She's sailed round the Galapagos Islands, camped in an Amazon rain forest, rafted through the Grand Canyon, horse-packed along the beaches of Isla Margarita, walked across volcanoes in Hawaii, and hiked in the Rocky Mountains. She's also visited Antarctica to marvel at penguins and icebergs, patted whales off Baja California, and most recently followed Isabella Bird's footsteps through northern Japan.

As a writer and journalist in England, she was the first woman reporter in the *Manchester Guardian*'s newsroom and was a reporter with Reuters News Agency in Paris. In the United States, her articles have been published in the *New York Times, Denver Post, McCalls, New Choices, New York, Travel & Leisure*, and other major publications. She is founder of Colorado Independent Publishers Association, past president of the American Society of Journalists and Authors, and conference director of the Colorado Magazine Writers Institute. She is listed in *Who's Who in America*. She lives in Boulder, Colorado, with her family.

CONTENTS

PREFACE

Jan Morris

Jan Morris has written some 35 books of history, travel, memoirs, and biography, most notably the Pax Britannica Trilogy about the rise and fall of the Victorian Empire, and a novel, Last Letters from Hav, *about an imaginary Mediterranean city. She is Welsh and lives in Wales.*

For better or for worse, I am one of those persons who, by some hormonal misunderstanding, began life in the male gender and moved on to the female. I lived adventurously as a man, and like everyone else, I used to suppose that this was because I had been subconsciously trying to prove my masculinity.

I have lately reached a different conclusion. I think now that when in those days I deliberately courted danger or discomfort, I was obeying not the masculine in me but the feminine. I have come to think that the female is intuitively more adventurous than the male.

The archetypal women-adventurers—"lady-adventurers" it would be perhaps be more proper to call them—were found among the upper-class daughters of Victorian England, if only because in their society women in general were particularly stifled by convention. Lady

Adapted from an article in Gourmet *magazine, January 2000. Reprinted with permission of the author.*

adventurers were generally childless. For most women of their time, childbirth was hazard enough, and the instinct to protect one's offspring dictated caution in life. Perhaps it was only when the Victorian bravas were excused (or denied) those grand responsibilities that their female instinct for adventure found its fulfilment. It was certainly no macho tendency in them. However rough and tough their lives, few of them abandoned the usual female preoccupations of their time and class, and they seldom wanted to appear dominant: resolute always, manipulative frequently, condescending sometimes, arrogant occasionally, bossy not often.

They famously disdained, of course—it is part of their legend— to wear trousers, even in the most demanding terrain. Isabella Bird, born in 1831 and one of the most widely traveled people of her day, was infuriated when a journalist claimed that on horseback she wore "masculine habiliments for greater convenience." He ought to be horse-whipped for the very suggestion, she thought: why, she wore a silk skirt and an elegant cloak even for her toughest riding expeditions! The explorer Mary Kingsley wore a high-necked white blouse, a cummerbund, and a long black skirt in the depths of the West African rain forests. Even Gertrude Bell the Orientalist, intellectually the most formidable of the lot, drooled over the hats sent to her in Baghdad by her London milliner.

Some of these women were married and journeyed with their husbands. They proved the most wifely of wives. "Not a screamer" is how Samuel Baker, the African explorer, described his wife, Florence; and a good thing, too, for she had plenty to scream about during her epic travels with him in the 1860s, looking for the source of the Nile. At times she was paralyzed by sunstroke or delirious with malaria, she was weakened by months of ox-back riding, and she once sank beneath the rotting weeds of the Kafue River. Once, a Bunyoro chieftain offered Samuel a nubile local virgin in exchange for her—a proposition hastily withdrawn when Florence rose from her sickbed and shattered the chief with invective. When in 1881 Lady Anne Blunt wrote a book about her intrepid travels in the Arabian peninsula, the frontispiece showed her traveling companion—her dear husband Wilfrid, dressed as a sheikh, holding a hunting hawk, and captioned "Portrait of Mr. Blunt."

Isabella Bird temporarily gave up traveling when she married, and when someone commiserated about a canceled trip to the East, she replied that, well, anyway, New Guinea was "not the sort of place you could take a man to."

Even the toughest of these characters were, of course, at times pursued by the usual complications of love. Miss Bird herself, a supremely self-possessed voyager, apparently lost her heart to Rocky Mountain Jim, a trapper and stock raiser of violent reputation and alcoholic tendencies. She described him as a lovable and terrible desperado, with a "wild eloquence that was truly thrilling," but emerged from this heady affair to wed a mild-mannered English country physician.

And surely nobody in the history of feminine emotion was more irresistibly animated by romantic love than Lady Jane Digby, who died in 1881. Sometime wife to an English earl and a German baron, this brilliant woman spent the last quarter century of her life blissfully wed to an Bedouin sheikh. She dressed like a Bedouin woman, blackening her eyelids with kohl, and once at least she rode camel-back into tribal battle (victoriously, of course). She died at 73, and her sad old husband sacrificed a camel in her honor. Sir Richard Burton, the explorer, said she was a woman "whose life's poetry never sank to prose."

It strikes me, though, that most of these women embarked upon their travels in a spirit that was less than poetical. Unlike men, they seldom set off into desert or bush just for the hell or the escape of it. Having embraced the impulse to live dangerously, they nearly always felt the need to transmute it into solid purpose.

Marianne North, for example, was a spinster flower-painter from Sussex. When in 1869 she was released from domestic responsibilities by the death of her widowed father, she threw herself into a mighty project to record the flora of the whole world. She was never strong, but nothing could deter her from her lonely travels. She lived in a hut deep in the rain forests to paint the tropical flowers of Brazil. She painted blossoms in the jungles of Borneo, in the mountains of Ceylon, all over India. She was a universal success—her paintings proving invaluable as a record of vanishing flora—and when she came to write her memoirs, she called them *Recollections of a Happy Life.*

Mary Kingsley was 30 and unmarried when both her parents died in 1893, freeing her from housekeeping. She upped and sailed away to West Africa, most of it unknown to foreigners, to investigate its ancient laws and religions, but over the subsequent years her interests greatly widened, and she became an expert on every aspect of West African society, history, fauna, and flora. Dressed always with decorous elegance, she seemed afraid of nothing. She paddled canoes through mangrove swamps full of crocodiles, taking soundings now and then with her furled umbrella. She hacked her way through forest accompanied only by half-naked indigenes. She slept in tribal huts and ate awful local food. Kingsley was among the first Europeans to get to know the West African tribes-people as fellow-humans. She liked them, and they liked her. To nearly everyone else West Africa was a hell-hole of ill-health, heat, fearful animals, and frightening people: to Mary Kingsley it was, in her own word, "charming."

Isabella Bird, too, was a decidedly purposeful adventurer. Among the most popular travel writers of her time, she was as observant as she was courageous, and often very funny. "There was never anybody," a London critic wrote, "who had adventures as well as Miss Bird," and to my mind this remains true to this day. She was the small and sickly daughter of a clergyman, but there was nowhere she would not go, nothing she would not do, for the sake of her craft. From the Japanese island of Hokkaido to the Hawaiian volcano Mauna Loa, from the Australian Outback to Tibet, Morocco and Korea, Armenia and Kashmir, Isabella Bird went almost everywhere and wrote about it all with indefatigable gusto.

I now believe that the most courageous, original and thoughtful adventurers have generally been women. Most of these Victorian ladies were more open-minded than their male contemporaries and more ready to adapt to foreign ways. When we read of women being especially daring—venturing alone into howling wildernesses, crossing limitless seas, climbing mountains of ghastly inaccessibility—they are demonstrating not the exception but the rule. It was Eve, after all, who plucked the apple in the Garden of Eden!

Introduction

I went to Japan because of Isabella Bird. This book is about our trips to Japan, separated by 120 years, and what we found. It's a literary pilgrimage and a personal adventure.

I discovered Isabella Bird when I found a book she wrote in 1873 about her visit to Colorado — and I was hooked. Here was a woman after my own heart. She loved to travel, enjoyed the outdoors and wilderness, welcomed the unusual and unexpected, and was a wonderful writer. When I moved to Colorado, I kept seeing the landscape through her eyes. She described the spectacular views of the Rocky Mountains from her cabin in Estes Park. She crossed the Continental Divide on her Indian pony through waist-high snow drifts. She climbed 14,000-foot Longs Peak and fell in love with her guide, Rocky Mountain Jim. But she decided that he drank too much and sailed home to Edinburgh to write *A Lady's Life in the Rocky Mountains*, the book I found which is still in print today.

Isabella Bird was one of those feisty Victorian lady travelers who went everywhere years before women went anywhere. Born in England in 1831, her ill health and bad back led her to doctors, who prescribed "a change of air." Usually ailing Victorian ladies went off to spend a week at the seashore or in the country. Bird used her doctor's advice as the excuse to take off for dozens of distant places.

Bird sailed to Japan in 1878, a few years after the country had just been opened to foreigners after more than 200 years of isolation. She arrived at the port of Yokohama, and then traveled north with her Japanese guide, Mr. Ito. It was a challenging trip on unpaved roads riding on a wooden saddle on Japanese horses. She marched through mountains, villages, and farmlands to the island of Hokkaido to find the primitive tribes of Ainu who were being persecuted by the Japanese.

Much of rural Japan was suffering from tremendous poverty. Because no foreigners had visited for 200 years, there were few facilities for travelers. Bird stayed in run-down inns, endured torrential rains that washed out roads and bridges, rode dozens of different horses, and dealt with fleas, mosquitoes, and innumerable other biting insects. She described every detail of her journey, and, realizing that many of the images would upset her readers' view of romantic Japan, explained: "The scenes are strictly representative. I offer them in the interests of truth. Accuracy has been my first aim."

After returning home from Japan, and writing her book, she took off for China, where she took a boat up the Yangtze River, and to Korea, where she met the king and queen, who did not impress her. Later, in Persia, she crossed the unexplored western desert with a revolver in her saddlebag, next to her packet of tea. When a group of bandits surrounded her, she noted: "I took my revolver out of the holster, and very slowly examined the chambers. The threatening tribesmen fell back, and began dispersing."

She was not a young woman when she began traveling. She took her first trip to Colorado in her forties, went to Japan in her fifties, and was in her sixties when she traveled through Asia. At age seventy, she rode through Morocco's Atlas Mountains on the Sultan's superb black horse. She died peacefully at home in Scotland at the age of seventy-three. Despite the unlikely places she visited, she always tried to preserve her image as a proper Victorian lady, though she wrote to a friend in Edinburgh: "I still vote civilization a nuisance, society a humbug, and all conventionality a crime."

Unlike other English travelers of her time, she did not believe that the world would be a better place if everyone behaved like the British, nor did she believe that Britain had a natural right to take over other countries as colonies. She was a devout Christian—her father had been a minister—but she still respected other religions and traditions, describing Buddhist temples and Hindu ceremonies in detail. And she did not hesitate to criticize when she felt it was justified. She was shocked by Japanese farmers working naked in the fields, disapproved of the harems she visited in Iran, and was outraged by Chinese officials who refused to let her travel farther. On a pilgrimage to climb Mount Sinai, she was horrified by the monks in St. Catherine's Monastery who pestered her to buy souvenirs. She refused to stay at the monastery and instead erected her tent in the desert in an effort to restore her peaceful mood of religious contemplation, and complained: "I almost wish I had abstained from visiting. How much of hollow mockery there is in their gorgeous church!"

She was always interested in the lives of women and children. In Japan, she was entranced by the well behaved children who played quietly and happily together without constant admonitions from their parents and wrote: "I have never yet heard a baby cry, and I have never seen a child troublesome or disobedient." In Tibet, she found that only the eldest son could marry, and he brought his bride to his parents' home. The other brothers then became secondary husbands, and the women explained: "If I had only one husband, and he died, I would be a widow. If I have two or three, I am never a widow!" In Korea, she wrote about the low status of Korean women, who, in one town, were only allowed to go outside their homes after dark.

Inspired by her travel books, I decided to write her biography. I researched her travels and her astonishing achievements. She was the author of ten books, the first woman Fellow of the Royal Geographical Society, and a Fellow of the Royal Scottish Geographical Society. In addition, long before British women could vote, she was invited to address British members of Parliament about her journey in Persia and was honored by being presented to Queen Victoria. My book, *Amazing Traveler Isabella Bird*, was first published in 1994 and in a second edition in 1999.

What drove Isabella Bird to travel? In the 1850s, a bright, intelligent woman in Britain had only one path available to her: to marry and depend on her husband. There were no schools for girls, no women's colleges, no opportunities for careers. Women were wives and mothers or lived with relatives. Only poor women were allowed to earn money doing menial labor. Indeed, it took a great deal of courage for Isabella and her sister, Henrietta, to live on their own after their parents died. Isabella earned enough money to support them, and Henrietta looked after the house. This was a very unusual arrangement in those days, and few women flouted convention by working to earn money to support themselves. Isabella realized that her ability to travel and write provided her only escape from the stifling regulations of polite Victorian society, which always made her sick and miserable. Indeed, her credo was: "Travelers are privileged to do the most improper things with perfect propriety."

Despite her energy and achievements, she was not beautiful, glamorous, or sexy. The few photos taken of her show a short, dumpy, rather plain woman looking directly at you with a serious expression. Her passion was travel, and she had the talent to write about it with accuracy, charm, amusement, and clarity. Her book about Hawaii, which she visited in 1872, has descriptions of surfing the waves and walking up fiery volcanoes that are as true today as when she saw them. She rode her horse across the countryside not sitting side-saddle, as Victorian ladies were supposed to, but astride, as Hawaiian women did, and told her sister: "I am doing what a woman can hardly ever do— leading a life fit for a man. Now with my horse and gear packed upon it, I need make no plans. I feel energy for anything except convention-ality and civilization."

Why have Isabella Bird and her travel books endured for more than a century? There were other travel writers at that time—she mentions them in her letters to friends—but their books have disap-peared. What she did brilliantly was to have incredible adventures on her travels and write about them with passion, wit, honesty, a sense of humor, and a slight touch of exaggeration. She never took a boring journey. No matter where she went, some disaster was sure to befall her. If she boarded a boat, it was sure to be tossed in a wild storm. If she went out in the winter, she would struggle through chest-high snow-drifts. If she traveled in summer, she would wilt in sweltering heat. Reading her books, I often wondered if everything really happened to her and came to the conclusion that once she started traveling, she saw everything through a prism of excitement, like rose-colored spectacles that dramatized every event. You or I might find a boat trip a little rough; Isabella Bird would describe torrents of water pouring over the decks, passengers clinging to poles in the dining room to avoid being swept overboard, deafening thunder shaking the heavens, and giant waves rearing above the boat.

In an era before photography and video cameras, Bird described everything in telling detail. Her dynamic descriptions show us vividly the places she saw, many of which have changed or disappeared. Her talent was her ability to write down exactly what she saw so that you feel as if you are standing next to her and experiencing it too, from her first afternoon in luxuriant tropical Hawaii to the exhilaration of climbing in the snow up the highest mountains in the Himalaya.

She also never took herself too seriously. She describes her struggle to mount a recalcitrant camel in the desert, killing cockroaches with her slippers in her cabin on a Pacific paddle steamer, and washing her hair in the Rocky Mountains on a day so cold that her braids froze to her head. Her voice rings clear and true as she journeys through snowstorms, torrential rain, scorching heat, and dripping humidity, rides a horse, camel, elephant, and yak, and travels by steamer, canoe, and raft.

The idea of following in her footsteps sounded a wonderful way to see Japan for the first time. I knew that I loved the kind of traveling she enjoyed, off the beaten track, and away from the tourists. With her book as my guide, I could follow her route to see what had changed. It would be a unique introduction to an unconventional view of Japan.

As I pored over maps, I realized her journey followed what is now the main route to the north, and it was easy to spot names of towns she visited and places she stayed. I would not travel on horse-back. Instead I would take trains and buses and bicycle or walk when I could. I too would stay in inns and small hotels, looking for Japanese places, and eating Japanese food along the way.

What I never expected to find was that her name is still alive and well, 120 years after her visit. On Hokkaido today, more than 24,000 descendants of the Ainu remain. By a lake in the town of Shiraoi in a beautifully reconstructed Ainu village of traditional straw huts, I met the museum director and dance choreographer. Both nodded emphatically when I mentioned Bird's name. Her book in Japanese was in the museum store.

In the village of Biratori, where Isabella Bird lived in a straw hut, a new museum elegantly displays Aino artifacts as well as videos of songs, stories, and dances. The director whipped out his copy of her book, and nodded emphatically as we talked about her travels. Farther south in Tajima, the Folklore Museum director rushed to find Bird's book on the shelf behind him; he writes scholarly articles for professional journals about her.

When Bird traveled through Yamagata in 1878, she was delighted with the rich, fertile farmlands and praised the area as "an Asiatic Arcadia." In 1984, an enterprising public official created the Arcadia Campaign, named after her comment, to preserve the environment and beautify the region. Three memorials to Bird have been erected in recent years with her quote in English and Japanese, and a local construction company calls itself "Isabera" after her.

In Nikko's old Kanaya Hotel, there are framed photos along the corridors of famous people who had stayed there—politicians, kings, queens, movie stars, sports figures, religious leaders—including one of Isabella Bird, with white hair, and wearing a flowing, dark dress.

Friends wondered why I didn't take my husband along on the trip. We've traveled together a great deal, but I realized that if I was going to follow the footsteps of a single woman on her own, I had to be a single woman on my own. Though that caused a certain amount of marital friction, once I had arrived in Japan, I knew it had been the right decision. Japan is a country where men are in power, and women are taught to take a subservient role. Had I traveled with my husband, no one would have spoken to me. They would have talked to him and expected him to take charge and tell me what to do. It would have been a completely different experience to the one I had and very different from Isabella Bird's.

Several people asked me what it was like to travel alone. Although I set out to travel on my own, I had guides to help me and contacts with people along the way. I was, in fact, traveling with Isabella Bird. She was a wonderful introduction to people I would never have met without her to guide me.

For me, it was truly astonishing to find that her original route led me to places where she was still remembered. I often felt as if she were traveling with me on the journey, nudging me to go where she knew there was something interesting, watching me when I went to places she did know, looking over my shoulder as I walked round museums, and nodding as I discovered the memorials to her. I had the sense that she wanted to make sure I found everything she thought I ought to see as we traveled together off the beaten track to find "the real Japan."

Chapter 1
Preparing for the Trip

He thinks my plan for traveling in the interior is rather too ambitious, but that it is perfectly safe for a lady to travel alone, and agrees with everybody else in thinking that legions of fleas and miserable horses are the great drawbacks of Japanese traveling.

Isabella Bird quoting advice from a British official, 1878

I think your itinerary is very wise. I wish I could go with you myself as your interpreter. As for the transportation, some people actually feel repulsive about the flawless punctuality of Japanese trains. If you are late by even ten seconds or so, it is almost guaranteed that your train has already gone, leaving you behind.

Advice in a letter to Evelyn Kaye from a Japanese tourist official, 1998

I sabella Bird went to Japan hoping to find interesting material for her next book. Her publisher, John Murray, had successfully published her book about Hawaii in 1875, and readers loved her adventurous stories about climbing an erupting volcano and riding through the pounding surf. Her magazine articles about her visit to Colorado Territory's Rocky Mountains in 1873 were equally popular, and John Murray hoped to publish them later as a book. Now she needed to find new material to write more articles and books.

She wrote to the British naturalist Charles Darwin, who had recently traveled in South America, to see if he thought it would be interesting to explore the Andes mountains on horseback, as she had done in Colorado. He did not recommend it. It was only when she talked to another British traveler and author, Constance Gordon Cummings, about her recent trip to Asia that she first heard of the changes taking place in Japan following the end of 200 years of isolation. Isabella Bird realized this might be a fascinating journey. When John Murray told her that two British male explorers were planning to travel there, and that he would love to have her book come out first, she decided to go and explore northern Japan, where few travelers had been. To protect her image as a proper Victorian lady, she asserted that she traveled to improve her health, because this was a time when single ladies were never expected to travel alone to find interesting material to write about or to enjoy the adventures of exploring new places.

In the preface of her Japan book, she wrote: "Having been recommended to leave home, in April 1878, in order to recruit my health, I decided to visit Japan, attracted less by the reputed excellence of its climate than by the certainty that it possessed, in an especial degree, those sources of novel and sustained interest which conduce so essentially to the enjoyment and restoration of a solitary health-seeker."

I went to Japan 120 years later for different reasons. Health was not one of them, but I too hoped to find interesting material to write about. I have traveled widely and have written about Antarctica, horse-packing trips, and traveling alone as well as guidebooks about educational travel and adventure vacations for women. I know Isabella Bird extremely well, having written her biography, traveled to many of the places she has visited, and admire her style of writing and travel. Now that I live in Colorado, it is fascinating for me to compare her descriptions of 1873 Colorado in her *Lady's Life in the Rocky Mountains* with the places I see today. I wondered what the other places she visited were like. By chance, I met several people who had lived and worked in Japan, and they were most encouraging about the idea.

As I studied Isabella Bird's route carefully from reading her book, I saw that, though place-names have changed and many of the villages have been absorbed into larger communities, it was easy to follow her path from Yokohama north through the mountain passes, across the plains and valleys, and by lakes and rivers. The geography was still the same, though modern roads and railways have replaced the old paths she took.

I was lucky because I could do almost all my research from my office in Colorado. My first surprise was that modern guidebooks rarely cover northern Japan in as much detail as the southern regions because fewer Western tourists travel there. It is, however, an extremely popular area for Japanese vacationers. I wrote to local Japanese tourist offices as well as the Japan National Tourist Office for information. I searched the Internet, visited bookstores and libraries, and talked to friends who have traveled or led tours in northern Japan. I planned to see national parks, lakes, canyons, and cliffs, visit farms and villages, and look for places of historic significance that Isabella Bird might have seen. Her route was very attractive to me because it avoided big cities and instead meandered through small towns and villages in the rural north of Honshu and on the island of Hokkaido.

A century earlier, Isabella Bird had few opportunities to learn about Japan before she left Scotland. She knew she would have to do her research once she arrived. Her long journey began with a train from Edinburgh to Liverpool, a ship across the Atlantic to New York, a train across the U.S. to San Francisco, and another ship across the Pacific where she spent "eighteen days of rolling over desolate rainy seas" before arriving at the port of Yokohama.

For the next few weeks, she consulted with officials and experts to learn as much as she could. Ernest Satow, the Secretary of the British Legation in Tokyo, was a renowned scholar and provided much of her information. She took his Anglo-Japanese dictionary with her, and later on her travels she noted: "When I asked educated Japanese questions concerning their history, religion, or ancient customs, I was often put off with the answer, 'You should ask Mr. Satow, he could tell you.'"

She decided to ride on horseback and go north through the interior. Once she reached the Tsugaru Straits, she would take a ferry to the island of Hokkaido, where she hoped to find the primitive tribes of Ainu. Other members of the British community offered advice. The scholar who had devised a system of Roman letters for the Japanese language, Dr. Hepburn, said she should not go because she would never make it. On the other hand, Sir Harry and Lady Parkes, the Consul and his wife, were much more encouraging. After Isabella Bird received an official map she had requested, she noticed that one section had been omitted, and an accompanying note explained that there was "insufficient information" about the area. Sir Harry looked at the map and said cheerily: "You will have to get your information as you go along, and that will be all the more interesting!"

She needed a special passport to travel in Japan, a document which she kept with her at all times and frequently had to show to officials. It allowed her to travel "for health, botanical research, or scientific investigation." She was forbidden to "light fires in woods, attend fires on horseback, trespass on fields, enclosures or game preserves, scribble on temples, shrines or walls, drive fast on a narrow road, or rent houses or rooms for a longer period than the journey requires."

Lady Parkes organized her luggage, which weighed 110 pounds and was to be carried by a packhorse. It was packed in two painted wicker boxes lined with paper and covered with waterproof covers of oiled paper. She had a folding canvas stretcher bed with wooden legs to keep her off the floor, away from the dreaded fleas. She took sheets and a blanket, a folding chair, an air-pillow, and a large rubber bath. In addition, she had a Mexican saddle and bridle, candles, a large map of Japan, and volumes of *Transactions of the English Asiatic Society*, which she took along as her guidebook.

She took few clothes. Her traveling dress was "a short costume of dust-colored striped tweed, with strong laced boots of unblacked leather." She purchased a traditional bowl-shaped Japanese hat with a white cotton cover and a light frame that allowed air to circulate beneath, noting: "It only weighs 2½ ounces, and is infinitely to be preferred to a heavy pith helmet, and, light as it is, it protects the head so thoroughly that no other protection has been necessary."

My luggage weighed 40 pounds altogether, enough for one person to carry, and was packed in a wheeled suitcase and a small daypack. The essentials for me were a Japanese-English dictionary, a phrase book, a guidebook, and two good maps. Friends advised me to take business cards translated into Japanese, which proved essential, and as souvenir gifts I brought some attractive Colorado keyrings and a few pens. I traveled in jeans, black walking sneakers, a long-sleeved cotton shirt, light sweater, heavy sweater, and a waterproof jacket with a hood so that I didn't need a hat. I was going in October when it was supposed to be cool. I packed a pair of black corduroy pants, light-weight tights and top to wear underneath if it was cold, three sweaters, two shirts, gloves, a pull-on hat, socks, a second pair of black sneakers, an umbrella, flip-flops, and a light robe.

Friends in the British community urged Isabella Bird to take food, warning her that she would not find bread, butter, milk, meat, poultry, coffee, wine, or beer on her travels, except at a few hotels for foreigners. She realized she had no room to carry the quantities of food they recommended and took only some raisins, chocolate, and brandy for emergencies. Later, she noted: "I should advise a person in average health—and none other should travel in Japan—not to encumber himself with tinned meats, soups, claret, or any eatables or drinkables."

In 1998, I was not worried about finding food in Japan. The only things I brought were some peppermints. Indeed, I was looking forward to tasting sushi, sashimi, sake, and other specialties I had enjoyed in Japanese restaurants in the United States.

Isabella Bird had no opportunity to book places to stay on her route, and knew she would have to trust to chance. I had lists of hotels and bed-and-breakfasts, and made advance bookings so that I had somewhere to stay almost every night. I was advised it was better to do this so I wouldn't have to make phone-calls at the last minute. Japanese hotels often simply say there is no room if they cannot understand a foreigner on the phone.

As writers, both Isabella Bird and I were prepared to take notes as we traveled. She took paper, pen and ink, and sent frequent letters to her sister, which provided the basis for her books. She kept a daily journal, a log of where and how far she traveled each day, and a notebook of jottings and ideas. She also had a sketchbook for drawings which were later used as the basis for the engravings that illustrated the Japan book.

I rejected the array of modern options of a laptop computer, daily e-mail, audio-tapes, and videotapes. The hassles of modern technology made me decide to keep it simple. I took pens and pencils, a large exercise book, a notebook with extra refill pages to clip in, and a small note pad. I would hand write a daily journal in the exercise book, use the notebook as a reporter does by putting down observations and interviews, and keep the pad handy for names, addresses, scribbled thoughts, ideas, suggestions to follow up, and on-the-spot reactions. I would also collect materials as I traveled, take lots of photos, and make sure I had names and addresses so I could check information later. My all-purpose camera was small enough to fit into my pocket, simple for me to operate, and sturdy enough to withstand the journey.

Isabella Bird and I both needed a guide. Neither of us spoke or read Japanese, and yet we wanted to learn and understand the country, its customs, and its people as we traveled through it for the first time. Through her friends at the Consulate, several candidates arrived for her to interview. She asked them questions in English and rejected those who couldn't understand her, or when they replied, she could not understand them. Finally she chose a young man of eighteen who said he had lived at the American Legation and had traveled through northern Japan with a British botanical collector. He added that he could walk twenty-five miles a day, cook a little, write English, and understood what the journey would be like. Most important, she could understand his English and he could understand her. Though he said his recommendations had been burned in a fire at his father's house, they immediately signed a contract for twelve dollars a month, and he requested a month's salary in advance, which she gave him.

She was relieved when he appeared the next morning punctually at the appointed hour, and found: "He seems as sharp or as smart as can be, and has already arranged for the first three days of my journey. His name is Ito. He has a large share of personal vanity, whitens his teeth, and powders his face carefully before a mirror, and is in great dread of sunburn. He powders his hands too, and polishes his nails, and never goes out with gloves. He flies up stairs and along the corridors as noiselessly as a cat, and already knows where I keep all my things. Nothing surprises or abashes him, and he is obviously quite at home in a Legation."

I had booked guides before I arrived but was not able to meet any of them beforehand. Through the Japan National Tourist Office, I learned about the 40,000 volunteer Goodwill Guides in towns and villages throughout Japan who take visitors on walking tours and provide information about what to see locally. The day-long service is free, though you are expected to buy your guide lunch. I requested guides for several places that were on the route, including Nikko, Aizu-Wakamatsu, Yamagata, and my last two days in Yokohama. From my research, I sent them each a prepared list of sights that sounded worth visiting. In return, I received a list of the guides' names and phone numbers, and when and where I should meet them. Most of them were called Mr. Ito, a common name in Japan!

On Hokkaido, when I would be looking for the Ainu, I wanted someone to help me with my research. So I hired a professional guide, Annette, an American woman who leads tours in Japan and who had lived there for seven years. We communicated by phone, fax, and e-mail, and signed a letter of agreement. We met for the first time when I reached Hokkaido.

Isabella Bird's first view of Japan was a dramatic glimpse of Mount Fuji. As the ship steamed up the coast: "I saw far above any possibility of height, a huge truncated cone of pure snow, 13,080 feet above the sea, from which it sweeps upwards in a glorious curve, very wan, against a very place blue sky, with its base veiled in a pale gray mist."

Her ship anchored out in Yokohama bay, and a flotilla of small boats ferried the passengers and their luggage to the quay. Isabella Bird took a *kurama*, a cart pulled by men, to the British Consulate, where officials whisked her off to her hotel.

My first view of Japan was Narita airport in Tokyo. I looked out of the window of the Japan Airlines plane in which I had been sitting for about ten hours. Through a thick bed of heavy, gray clouds, I saw below the black shiny asphalt of a rain-slick runway. I tried to feel excited, thinking "This is Japan, and I have never been here before." But excitement was hard to muster. The feeling I had was a passionate desire to get off the plane, stop moving, and breathe some real air. I desperately wanted to lie down somewhere quiet and horizontal and sleep. I worried about being able to find my way around, getting through customs, finding a taxi to my hotel, finding my room. I wondered why air travel was so tiring when all you do is sit. I asked myself why I had come, whether it had all been a terrible mistake, and if I was about to spend the three worst weeks of my life in Japan when I could have stayed quietly at home.

The plane finally landed and taxied through the rain to the gate. I lifted down my suitcase, put on my daypack, and followed the other passengers out into an airport building that looked just like most other airport buildings. All the signs were in English and Japanese. Arrows clearly pointed the way. The friendly customs inspector gave my things a cursory glance and wished me a good visit. I chose a taxi from the line of them outside the exit doorway, and the driver nodded politely and took me quickly to the hotel.

The city streets were filled with traffic lights, cars, buses, trucks, and neon signs. Except for a few signs with the squiggly letters of Japanese, it looked very much like city streets in any part of the world, though, unlike America, the traffic ran on the left-hand side of the road so I felt as if I'd arrived in London.

At the hotel, everyone spoke English, the elevator took me to my floor, I found my room and fell into bed with relief. Tomorrow I would travel to the historic town of Nikko, meet my Goodwill Guide, and visit the magnificent shrines that have stood unchanged for centuries.

Chapter 2
Nikko

The Nikko shrines are the most wonderful work of their kind in Japan. They take one prisoner by their beauty, in defiance of all rules of western art, and compel one to acknowledge the beauty of forms and combinations of color hitherto unknown.

Isabella Bird, 1878

Nikko well deserves to be one of the most popular day trips from Tokyo, but to beat the crowds, consider turning it into a three-day trip. Spend a night, see Nikko in the early morning, then push on into the interior of Nikko National Park.
Gateway to Japan, *1998 edition*

Never say 'kekko' (content) until you have seen Nikko.
Japanese saying

On June 10, 1878, the day she set off for Nikko, three days journey north, Isabella Bird admitted: "I have suffered from nervousness all day—the fear of being frightened, of being rudely mobbed, of giving offence by transgressing the rules of Japanese politeness—of I know not what!"

Once she set out, she felt better, bowling merrily over bumpy roads in a *kurama* pulled by men, past farms and rice-fields, through the flat countryside north of Tokyo. But her first night in a Japanese inn confirmed her worst fears. The matting on the floor of her room was thick with fleas, mosquitoes attacked her, and the canvas on her folding bed broke. Through the paper screens round her room, she heard other guests talking, bathing, singing, and playing musical instruments. To her horror, she saw curious guests even poked holes in the screens to peer at her. Suddenly, two policemen arrived, demanding that she show them her passport. After they left, she stayed awake for the rest of the night.

She wrote the next day: "Already, I can laugh at my fears and misfortunes. A traveler must buy his own experiences, and success or failure depends mainly on personal idiosyncracies. Lack of privacy, bad smells, and the torments of fleas and mosquitoes are, I fear, irremediable evils."

But her stay the second night at another inn was even noisier and more uncomfortable. In addition to the fleas, insects, and screens with holes, she found the servants coming into her room on any pretext, and there was a continuous din of musicians playing, girls singing, drums beating, and storytellers reciting so that she could not sleep at all. She confessed: "I nearly abandoned Japanese traveling altogether, and, if last night in Nikko had not been a great improvement, I think I should have gone ignominiously back to Tokyo."

As she approached Nikko, "the country became prettier and prettier, rolling up to abrupt wooded hills with mountains in the clouds behind. As the day wore on in its brightness and glory, the pictures became more varied and beautiful. Great snow-slashed mountains looked out over the foothills, on whose steep sides the dark blue green pine and cryptomeria was lighted up by the spring tints of deciduous trees."

In Nikko, she rented a room with the Kanaya family and was elated to find "a Japanese idyll; there is nothing within or without which does not please the eye, and after the din of the inns, its silence, musical with the dash of waters and the twitter of birds, is truly refreshing. It is a simple but irregular two-storied pavilion, standing on a stone-faced terrace approached by a flight of stone steps. The garden is well laid out, and, as peonies, irises, and azaleas are now in blossom, it is very bright."

Her room had a light wood ceiling and panels of sky-blue paper sprinkled with gold. The fine matting was white and perfectly clean. In an alcove with polished wood floors stood a single spray of rose azalea in a pure white vase. Her supper that night arrived on a small lacquered table with rice served in a gold lacquer bowl and tea in a fine porcelain teapot and cup.

"I almost wish that the rooms were a little less exquisite," she confessed, "for I am in constant dread of spilling the ink, indenting the mats, or tearing the paper windows."

Kanaya and his sister talked about their dream of building a hotel for foreign visitors. Today, the Kanaya Hotel, one of Nikko's elegant old hotels, is well known. Unfortunately, it was completely booked on the days I was there.

It was pouring with rain when I reached Nikko after a journey of a couple of hours on one of Japan's fast trains. Instead of walking, I took a taxi to Pension Turtle, relieved that the taxi driver understood where I wanted to go. My room at the pension, on a quiet side street by the river, was clean and neat, with a carpet, two single beds against the walls, hooks for clothes on the wall, and a Western-style bathroom with a shower and flush toilet. On the shelf opposite the door was large TV set. The curtained windows looked out on a sheltered garden. As I started unpacking, there was a knock on the door. A smiling young woman brought me a cup of tea and a tourist map of Nikko.

I sipped the tea and decided to go out for some food. A light drizzle fell as I strolled up the narrow, cobbled street alongside the Daiyagawa river which was rushing by, full from the rain. On either side were plain, two-story houses set behind stone walls and hedges. Cars were parked at odd angles in driveways, but there was little traffic. A woman passed me and nodded her head politely, and I smiled at her. I turned right to climb a steep hill and came out on a busy main road with buses and cars.

On the corner was a local supermarket, bright with neon lights and colorful posters. As I wandered down the aisles, I studied the pictures on cans and packages and guessed the flavors of bottles of juice and soda. In the refrigerator section sat a stack of sushi dinners in trays, just like those in American supermarkets. I picked one, chose a bottle of juice and a packet of cookies, and paid at the counter. The clerk changed the note and gave me a collection of coins.

Back in my cozy room, I turned on the TV, which needed coins to make it work, settled comfortably on the bed, and dunked the sushi in soy sauce and mustard. I watched a baseball game, which I could understand perfectly, a talk show, which was quite beyond me, the movie *The King and I* with Yul Brynner and Japanese subtitles, and the weather channel, with neat icons for sun, clouds, and rain. I fell asleep listening to the rain dripping on the roof.

Nikko has been famous for its shrines since 1617 when shogun Tokugawa Ieyasu, one of the most powerful leaders in Japanese history, was buried here in Tosho-gu, now a magnificent park with memorial temples and shrines. His elaborate funeral procession is re-enacted every year. In 1634, his grandson, Tokugawa Iemitsu, invited more than 15,000 artisans from all over Japan to create ornate temples, buildings, and sculptures as a memorial. Iemitsu wanted the Toshu-gu to be so ornate and costly that no other lord would ever be able to rival it. The project was said to have cost 568,000 ryo of gold, 800 pounds of silver, and 1,000 koku of rice—estimated at more than $200 million in today's dollars. When Iemitsu died in 1653, he was buried nearby.

Isabella Bird set off for the shrines from the Kanaya's house, first crossing the river by the Sacred Bridge, built in 1636. She commented: "There is nothing imposing in its structure," and I would not argue with her. Legend says that when the Buddhist priest Shodo arrived in 776 and wanted to cross the Daiyagawa river, there was no bridge. He recited a Buddhist sutra, and an old man in white clothes with a long white beard appeared on the opposite side, hurled two snakes, one red and one green, across the river, and the snakes were transformed into a bridge. In 1902, a storm knocked the old bridge down and it was rebuilt and painted in red lacquered vermilion.

She walked to the shrine entrance along a wide avenue lined with trees, "a broad road with steps at intervals and stone-faced embankments on either side," and saw "at the summit of this ascent is a fine granite *torii* gate, offered by the lord of Chikuzen in 1618 from his own quarries. On the left is a five-storied pagoda, 104 feet high, richly carved in wood and as richly gilded and painted. The signs of the zodiac run round the lower story."

Today, the wide avenue still leads to the entrance, and the trees are now grown high and thick. The entrance is through a granite *torii* gate, one of the largest in Japan. Stone steps lead into the first courtyard where the pagoda stands, now freshly painted in vivid dark red, deep turquoise, and black. The edges of the five square roofs are embellished with gold leaf. Fanciful carvings sit under the eaves. Today, the trees around are as tall as the building.

The twelve Chinese zodiac signs, three on each side, are easy to see. At the top of the pagoda is a hollyhock symbol, representing the Tokugawa family emblem, and around the topmost roof are carved symbols of the tiger, the rabbit, and the dragon, representing the years that the first, second, and third shogun were born. The pagoda's unique design has no central pillar because the building is suspended from the fourth floor to protect it from earthquakes.

"The grand entrance gate is at the top of a handsome flight of steps, forty yards from the *torii*," she noted. "The view of the first court overwhelms one by its magnificence and beauty. The whole style of the buildings, the arrangements, the art of every kind, the thought which inspires the whole, are exclusively Japanese."

The ornately decorated entrance gate is still at the top of a flight of steps. As you go through it, there is a wonderful sense of entering a different world. On the left side Isabella Bird saw "a sumptuous stable, for the sacred Albino horses, which are kept for the use of the god, a magnificent cistern of holy water, fed from the Somendaki cascade, and a highly decorated building, in which a complete collection of Buddhist scriptures is posited."

Today, in a beautifully decorated stable, stands one perfect white horse with a flowing mane. Koha, a gift from the Maori people as a token of goodwill and friendship between Japan and New Zealand, was busy munching some grass hay in his feeder. This was his day on duty while his two horse-mates relaxed in a pasture awaiting their turn to be stared at by visitors and have their photos taken.

Just above the entrance to the stable is a panel showing the famous Three Wise Monkeys, who hear no evil, see no evil, and speak no evil. The lively figures are carved and painted in turquoise, brown, white, and gold.

Many other countries sent gifts for the lavish memorial, and Isabella Bird saw a crouching stone lion from China, three lanterns from the Netherlands, and an elegant bronze bell from Korea, which are all still there. She described "a magnificent granite cistern," and there is a stone water fountain, fed from local streams, so visitors can wash hands and mouth before entering the temples. The Rinzo library building, with its collection of Buddhist literature, still stands at one side, and now charges an entrance fee.

The stunning difference between Isabella Bird's visit and mine was that she and Ito were alone. From the moment I arrived, I was surrounded by a sea of tourists, even on the weekday in October when I visited. Walking along the approach on the main avenue was like maneuvering among crowds on a New York City street.

Men, women, and children of all ages walked along the avenue, stopped and stared at the sights, talked, and took photographs constantly. Clumped around their teachers, groups of schoolchildren pushed forward, dressed in a variety of uniforms, some in yellow caps, some in blue, others wearing navy jackets, others wearing red blazers. Adult groups were led by guides in neat uniforms that included white gloves, and each leader held up a handkerchief-size flag on a stick with the group's name and title. Men in business suits and ties walked briskly along the paths. Clusters of foreign tourists, clutching guidebooks and looking bewildered, stared at the buildings. Parents pointed out sights to young children as they walked over the uneven cobbles. A gaggle of teenage girls in short skirts and high heels skipped along, giggling together. A group of older women strolled by slowly, pausing to talk and laugh. Most of the faces looked Japanese or Asian, though there were a few Europeans and Americans. People's shoes clicked and clacked on the cobbles, voices talked, called, and cried, and noise was an incessant background.

Isabella Bird's guide to the shrines was Ito. She found him "so clever that he is now able to be cook, laundryman, and general attendant, as well as courier and interpreter. He is intensely Japanese, and he thinks everything inferior that is foreign. Our manners, eyes, and modes of eating appear simply odious to him. Nominally, he is a Shintoist, which means nothing. At Nikko, as I read to him the story of the Prodigal Son, I was interrupted by a somewhat scornful laugh and the remark, 'Why, all this is our Buddha over again!'"

An old priest showed her around one temple and shocked her by pointing to some religious symbols, saying: "We used to believe in these things, but we don't now," in a manner she found "rather contemptuous." She knew Japan had recently passed laws declaring Shinto as Japan's national religion, which led to the destruction of many Buddhist buildings and art treasures. She noticed that one shrine was "shorn of all its glories of ritual, and its magnificent Buddhist paraphernalia; the 200 priests who gave it splendor are scattered, and six Shinto priests alternately attend upon it as much for the purpose of selling tickets of admission as for any priestly duties."

I set off early the next morning to walk to the train station to meet my Goodwill Guide for the day. Mr. Ito was a retired teacher of English whose passion was studying the shrines. At the information counter, I saw him talking to a woman traveler. At first glance, my heart sank. He was very short, wizened, and wrinkled, and had a round hat squished on top of his head. He wore thick, owlish glasses, his large ears stuck out, and he didn't have much hair. He wore a light blue rain-jacket, khaki pants, and black walking shoes, with a fanny-pack clipped round his waist. He reminded me of Mr. Magoo, the cartoon character.

But as soon as we walked through the historic stone entrance gate to the shrines, Mr. Ito was transformed. The subdued old man became a passionate historian, alive, alert, and determined to tell me every detail about the shrines, and to share the stories, legends, and facts that had taken him a lifetime to learn. He pointed out dragons lurking on lanterns, Confucius among the carved Chinese figures, barrels of sacred sake and whiskey, a dragon on the ceiling whose eyes followed you, engraved hollyhocks in unlikely places which were emblems of the shogun, white paint made from seashells, angels singing on the ceiling of an arch, a rabbit on top of a doorway, a sleeping cat, the different expressions of the lions, the variety of patterns. His enthusiasm was so contagious that I found myself taking notes frantically, shooting dozens of photographs, and hardly noticing the hours as they sped by.

Isabella Bird was absolutely overwhelmed by the magnificence of the Yomei Gate, or Yomei-mon. She enthused: "The white columns which support it have capitals formed of great red-throated heads of the mythical beasts, the *kirin*. Above is a projecting balcony which runs all around the gateway with a railing carried by dragons' heads. In the center two white dragons fight eternally. Underneath, in high relief, there are groups of children playing, then a network of richly painted beams, and seven groups of Chinese sages. The high roof is supported by gilded dragons' heads with crimson throats."

The gate has not changed. It stands magnificent and imposing, repainted and gilded, and photographed constantly. The spectacular gateway symbolizes the brilliance of Nikko, a name that can mean "sunny splendor" or the "sun's rays." You approach the gate by a long flight of wide stone steps. White pillars stand in a line at the front. Each one has been carefully painted in a different pattern. One pillar has the design upside down, on purpose. The belief is you never want to complete your building perfectly because, once it is finished, it starts to fall apart.

The pillars frame two massive wooden doors. Above them is a balcony, and above that is a high peaked tiled roof. Every available inch of the walls and ceilings between them is decorated with figures, painted engravings, animals, dragons, and paintings in vivid colors.

One series of eight beautifully sculptured scenes shows stories from Chinese mythology and history. A group of figures depicts the mother of Lao Tse who, concerned about her son's education, leaves home so she can live near a school. Another shows Confucius with his disciples looking at a river, which symbolizes the continuity of life, birth, and death. Mr. Ito could not explain a scene of the Emperor of China surrounded by smiling assistants watching as he washed his hair and made decisions at the same time, though perhaps my English and Mr. Ito's Japanese didn't quite communicate.

Isabella Bird's accurate drawing shows the imposing decorated gate with the wide steps leading up to it. One person stands on the top step, dwarfed by the looming edifice, to show the scale. Isabella Bird came several times to look at the Yomei-mon and wrote: "I contemplated its splendor day after day with increasing astonishment."

Today, contemplation is rare. The wide steps are constantly filled with people going up and down, standing, looking, pointing, lifting children up to see, photographing, talking, and pushing. There was nowhere I could stand to replicate the peaceful view Isabella Bird drew in her book. The photograph I have is filled with the backs of people's heads.

The cemetery where the inspiration for the shrine, Tokugawa Ieyasu, is buried is not amid the grandeur of the temples and shrines but behind them on the mountainside up a long, wide flight of steps beautifully cut out of gray stone. The stairway leads in a curving climb to the graves. The steps are edged with carved stone walls covered with soft green moss and shaded by tall, old cedar trees. Isabella Bird admired the masonry of the walls and steps, put together without mortar or cement, "and so accurately fitted that the joints are scarcely affected by the rain, damp, and aggressive vegetation of 260 years."

Today, there are engraved signs along the way with sayings such as: "Life is like going a long distance with heavy steps," and "Stop and rest," and "Don't make haste in leading your life." Here too, a constant stream of people walked up and down, counted the steps aloud as they walked, or paused to rest and talk.

At the top, encircled by a metal fence, stands the simple tomb of stone and bronze. On display is an imposing incense burner, a gift from the king of Korea, and a life-size statue of a bronze crane standing on a turtle, symbols of life. Isabella Bird commented on the silence and sense of mourning that surround the grave. Today, the voices of visitors and clicking of cameras are a constant refrain.

Nearby, she visited two temples which still stand, and she saw: "The roof of the hall is paneled and richly frescoed. The shogun's room contains some *kirin* depicted on a dead gold ground, and four oak panels, finely carved."

Today, the room is decorated with paintings of a hundred dragons, each one with a different — and more terrifying — expression. An adjoining room, where the shogun would rest before praying to his forefathers, was also decorated and painted, with poems and pictures in frames around the walls.

Even here, crowds jostled into the temple, and there was a perpetual buzz of voices, people, and activity. I edged into a large room down a couple of steps in the back of a temple, where everyone sat on the floor. Silence fell when a woman Shinto priest came on to the platform, her dark hair smoothed back, her face smooth and impassive. She was dressed in a flowing white robe from neck to ankles, with floating panels of lightweight red fabric. Mr. Ito translated her brief talk, explaining the significance of the temple, demonstrating how to pray at a shrine—bow twice, clap hands, make a wish—and urging us to buy charms at the counter as we left, which Mr. Ito said weren't worth the money.

As we left, I noticed two sculptures which had also attracted Isabella Bird's attention. She described the God of the Wind and the God of Thunder: "Wind has crystal eyes and a half-jolly, half-demoniacal expression. He is painted green, and carries a wind-bag on his back, a long sack tied at each end, with the ends brought over his shoulders and held in his hands. The god of thunder is painted red, with purple hair on end, and stands holding thunderbolts in his hand."

The two dramatic figures still stand today. Wind looks like a wrestler with a long snaking wind-bag around his shoulders. His muscular upper body and his thick arms and hands are painted a dark red with blue-green highlights. His face has a ferocious expression, with round painted red circles on his cheeks, nose, and chin, and black shapes on his forehead and cheeks. Tied loosely round his hips is a robe which has faded almost to white, though there are traces of turquoise, gold, and black patterns. The God of Thunder is equally terrifying, painted dark red with a malevolent expression on his face, and a raised thunderbolt in his left hand. Both of them are magnificently powerful figures, their eyes bold and fierce, daring you to challenge them.

Nearby, carved and painted flowers that Isabella Bird described in detail are still visible, and I too was fascinated by the rich, lush blossoms erupting into perfect bloom with a sensuous voluptuousness that you could almost feel. She wrote: "The lotus leaf retains its dewy bloom, the peony its shades of creamy white, the bamboo leaf still trembles on its graceful stem, and countless corollas, in all the perfect coloring of passionate life, unfold themselves amidst the leafage of the gorgeous tracery."

Finally, Isabella Bird felt she had seen enough. "To pass from court to court is to pass from splendor to splendor. One is almost glad to feel that this is the last, and that the strain on one's capacity for admiration is nearly over." Later she added: "The details fade from my memory daily as I leave the shrines, and in their place are picturesque masses of black and red lacquer and gold, gilded doors opening without a sound, halls laid with matting so soft that not a footfall sounds, walls and panels carved with birds and flowers, and on ceilings paneled and wrought with elaborate art, of inner shrines of gold, and gold lilies six feet high, and curtains of gold brocade, and incense fumes, and colossal bells."

I too felt flooded by the deluge of images, colors, shapes, carvings, sculptures, paintings, and details of this magnificent work of art. As I walked on through gateways and courtyards, the unending display of imposing temples, sculptured shrines, carved stone gates, monumental stone tombs, and dazzling decorations in purple, violet, orange, and green, black, white, gold, and silver was overwhelming. Every corner was decorated with representations of bizarre animals and horrendous monsters, cruel devils and fire-breathing dragons, awe-inspiring gods and legendary figures from Asian mythology. I found myself lulled into a half-hypnotized state, allowing the sights to flow over me, unable to absorb anything more.

I was relieved when Mr. Ito took me to see shrines in the mountains that reflected simplicity rather than opulence. The mountains have been a sacred place for more than 1,200 years since Shodo, the Buddhist priest who crossed the Sacred Bridge, came to the area in 766. He was followed by others who settled in the mountains to spread Buddhist teachings.

In a quiet, tree-shaded glen surrounded by low shrubs and wildflowers I saw Shodo's memorial tombstone covered with green moss. Nearby stood a plain, square temple building where, once a year, monks wearing traditional black and white robes attend a special service. The only sound was rain dripping from the trees. Around were tall brooding pines, their trunks almost black from the rain. A pungent scent of pine needles and damp earth filled the air. A stone footbridge led over a rushing, narrow stream, and a thin, white waterfall tumbled over the rocks. There were no tourists, no crowds, no guides. For the first time, I understood why Buddhist monks had settled in the mountains to find peace for religious contemplation.

As Isabella Bird had done, I ended the day at the Kanaya Hotel. Overlooking the Sacred Bridge by the river, it's a charming building with a long low veranda. As you walk in through the main door into the lobby, there's a welcoming ambience, like a family home. The down-stairs lounge has comfortable armchairs and sofas grouped round low tables. Large windows look out on a gracefully sculptured Japanese garden, the statues and gray stones shining in the rain. I ordered coffee and the hotel specialty, which was a round chocolate cake with raisins and rum.

Afterwards, I wandered along the corridors admiring the framed photographs of famous visitors who have stayed at the hotel since it opened more than a century ago. They represent an extraordinary collection of politicians, presidents, kings, queens, and princesses, authors, millionaires, inventors, musicians, movie stars, sports figures and others from around the world. It was like walking through history.

In the lobby, just as I was leaving, I glanced at the photographs hanging opposite the registration desk. I stopped in astonishment. There was a superb photograph of Isabella Bird, standing serene and elegant. She wore white ruffles at her throat and wrists, and a formal black dress in shiny material with a tight waist, and wide skirt. Her white hair was swept up in a flattering style, and her hands were folded calmly in front of her. Her face looked relaxed, with that direct gaze I knew so well, looking out at all who passed. She had been hanging there on the wall, waiting for the right moment to catch my attention, to remind me she too had visited Nikko, 120 years ago.

Chapter 3
Tajima and Aizu

The large town of Wakamatsu stands near the southern end of the plain, and it is sprinkled with many towns and villages. The great lake of Iniwashiro is not far off. The plain is rich and fertile. In the distance the steep roofs of its villages, with their groves, look very picturesque.

Isabella Bird, 1878

Northward bound travelers have to make a side trip around Lake Inawashiro to reach the inland city of Aizu-Wakamatsu, but the old castle town with so much of its past still preserved is worth the special effort. It was the capital of the Aizu clan. The Tsuruga castle was first erected in 1384. Today, even though it supports a population of 110,000, the city prides itself on its history.

Jan Brown, Exploring Tohuku, *Weatherhill, 1982*

Leaving Nikko, Isabella Bird set off north through the mountains to Tajima and Aizu on her first packhorse. The pony-size mare, with a shaggy mane and forelock, walked along behind a woman holding a rope tied round the animal's nose. The woman tied straw sandals on its feet over stony or slippery ground.

The saddle was made of two thick packs of straw, fitted at the ends with painted wood arches, with a padded quilt set on top, and a rope girth tied loosely under the horse's belly. The only way to mount was to drop down from a wall, and Isabella Bird found, "I was then fourteen inches above the animal's back, with my feet hanging over his neck. If the horse does not stumble, the pack-saddle is tolerable on level ground, but most severe on the spine in going up hill, and so intolerable in going down that I slid over the horse's head into a mud-hole."

Her route took her along "a most atrocious trail that wound about among the round boulders of the Daiya river, which it crosses often on temporary bridges of timbers covered with branches and soil. After crossing one of the low spurs of the Nikkosan mountains, we wound among ravines whose steep sides are clothed with maple, oak, magnolia, elm, pine. Every vista was blocked by some grand mountain, waterfalls thundered, bright streams glanced through the trees, and in the glorious sunshine, the country looked most beautiful." The pony ambled along, often going slower than a mile an hour.

"Comfort was left behind at Nikko!" she exclaimed when she arrived at a village for her first night's stay. It was "a very poor place, with poverty-stricken houses, children very dirty and sorely afflicted with maladies, and women with complexions and features hardened by severe work and much wood smoke into positive ugliness." In addition, she noted that "the men may be said to wear nothing. Few of the women wear anything but a short petticoat wound tightly round them, or blue cotton trousers very tight in the legs and baggy at the top, with a blue cotton garment open to the waist tucked into the band, and a blue cotton handkerchief knotted round the head. The houses were all poor, and the people dirty both in their clothing and person. I can hardly believe myself to be in civilized Japan."

Her room in the next village was above the kitchen and stable. She sat down to write but was forced to sit on the balcony because of bites from the fleas on the floor mats. "Cobwebs hung from the uncovered rafters. The mats were brown with age and dirt, the rice was musty, and only partially cleaned, the eggs had seen better days, and the tea was musty. Beetles, spiders, and woodlice held a carnival in my room after dark, and fleas rendered sleep impossible. At five Ito came and entreated me to leave, whimpering, 'I've had no sleep—there are thousands and thousands of fleas!' The night was very long."

Concerned that her readers who held romantic views of Japan might not believe her experiences, she added: "I write the truth as I see it, and if my accounts conflict with those of tourists who write of the Tokaido and Nakasendo, of Lake Biwa and Hakone, it does not follow that either is inaccurate. But truly this is a new Japan to me, of which no books have given me any idea, and it is not fairyland."

The next day she walked for five miles in pouring rain and admired the "high mountains, gloriously wooded and cleft by dark ravines, down which torrents were tumbling in great drifts of foam, crashing and booming, multiplied by many an echo, and every ravine afforded glimpses far back of more mountains, clefts and waterfalls, and such over-abundant vegetation I welcomed the sight of a gray cliff or bare face of rock. The spring tints have not yet darkened into the monotone of summer, rose azaleas still light the hillsides, and masses of cryptomeria give depth and shadow. I do not expect to see anything lovelier in Japan."

That night, she was given the best room in the Express Agent's office, with high ceilings, shiny dark wood walls and floor, and soft, clean mats, and "it is luxury after last night," she commented. But the inn they reached the following night was thick with smoke, with rafters blackened from soot and moisture. There was nothing to eat but black beans and boiled cucumbers.

As she traveled farther north, she faced a new problem. Every time she entered a town, she became the center of attention. "In these little-traveled districts, as soon as one reaches the margin of a town, the first person one meets turns and flies down the street, calling out the Japanese equivalent of 'Here's a foreigner!' Soon blind and seeing, old and young, clothes and naked, gather together. These Japanese crowds, however, are quiet and gentle, and never press rudely on one."

The day I left Nikko, I glanced up as I packed my things in the Pension Turtle and saw sheets of water streaming down my window. It was pouring with rain, the advance deluge of an approaching typhoon. Rivers of water sloshed through the streets during the drive to the railroad station.

When the train pulled out, I saw distant mountain peaks almost hidden in clouds and gray mist. A heating vent below my seat warmed my legs and feet. Above the windows, rows of colorful advertisements displayed wedding couples posing in front of flowers and lakes in dazzling sunshine in Nikko.

The train chugged off. We passed white plastered houses with square windows and shutters, and curved tiled roofs. The persimmon trees were laden with large orange fruit and bent over, their leaves dark and green. A splash of color came from a four-storied apartment building painted bright blue, its rows of metal balconies draped with clothes hung out to dry.

In the corner of a field stood a graveyard with stone shrines and memorials. Other fields rushed by, green with rice growing in neat rows. Beyond, steep slopes thick with dark trees and bushes disappeared into the low clouds. As we passed through a ravine, a dense grove of evergreens crowded close to the train on either side of the track. The trees were so tightly packed that their tall black trunks looked like a prison fence. We came out into a valley with fields, some bare with dark brown earth neatly ploughed, and some green with fresh plants. A wide bridge took us over a rushing river, the water foaming over rocks along its path. A line of electricity pylons marched toward the horizon. A new farmhouse covered in white stucco sparkled in the gray air.

As my train rushed past the scenery at about 70 miles an hour, in contrast to Isabella Bird's pace as she jogged along on her horse, I looked at my fellow travelers, all Japanese. Though I was the only foreigner on the train, no-one stared or took any notice of me. The man opposite, in a dark gray business suit, white shirt, and dark tie, had a tense, round face, and thinning dark hair. From his shiny leather briefcase, he took a calculator, some sheets of paper and a pen, and jotted down a series of numbers on the margin of the first page. Then he looked up, sniffed loud and hard first through one nostril, then the other, several times, and then bent his head rapidly from one side to the other, as if clearing his ears. He returned to his calculations, stopped, sniffed, and bent his head, and repeated the procedure several times. I wondered if he had a meeting with his boss about a major financial disaster, or if he did this every morning on the way to work.

Two young women in the corner took no notice of him. One of them, her bright purple hair cut in spikes, was talking animatedly, giggling and gesturing. She wore a close-fitting brown turtleneck sweater, wide-legged beige pants with perfect pleats, and a pair of black shoes with clunky four-inch heels. Her friend, listening politely, had on tight white jeans, a cranberry red sweater, and a pair of navy sneakers. Suddenly a musical sound rang out. Purple Hair clumsily opened her suitcase-size shiny white shoulder-bag, and took out a cellular phone decorated with jingling ornaments. Talking loudly, she walked to the end of the carriage and stood in the outer lobby, sliding the door closed behind her. Her friend watched and sighed.

My train arrived in Aizu-Wakamatsu station after a couple of hours. Warm sunshine poured down outside the station as I looked round for my next Goodwill Guide, Nina. I noticed a smiling woman walking toward me. I said: "Hi, I'm Evelyn. Are you a Goodwill Guide?" She replied in English with a North American twang: "Yes, I'm Nina."

Nina, a Canadian, had spent two years teaching in Japan. She now worked for an international association and loved showing people around. I was exhilarated to be able to speak English again, and astonished at what a relief it was not to struggle with my pseudo-Japanese or to find simple English phrases. The loss of language when you travel is a major deprivation, and I was so happy to be talking to someone who understood everything I said. She took me for a *ramen* noodle lunch in a restaurant filled with Japanese people, and we discussed what I wanted to do. We agreed she would show me the sights around Aizu, and then we'd drive to Tajima, where she lived, in the mountains.

From the noodle restaurant near the railroad station, we drove along the main road through Aizu-Wakamatsu. I was disappointed that Aizu looked so ordinary. The steady traffic was made up of Toyotas and

Hondas, as well as buses, bicycles, and trucks. The wide roadways had paved sidewalks where people in suits and jeans and skirts and jackets walked along purposefully. There were shoe stores, office building, garages, flower shops, restaurants, and parking lots. Aizu looked like Denver or Boston or almost any American town with traffic, storefronts, office buildings, department stores, and even—much to my surprise— a Denny's restaurant. Despite the Japanese faces on the streets, everything looked much too familiar.

Aizu's most famous sight is a reminder of a tragedy. Iimoriyama, set on a hill overlooking the city, is a memorial to the suicides of 19 samurai teenagers, aged fourteen to seventeen. Members of the White Tiger Brigade fighting their first battle in the Boshin Civil War in 1868, they were forced to retreat to the hill. Looking out, they saw smoke and fire around Tsurugajo Castle, the home of their samurai lord. They assumed that he had been defeated and killed. The samurai code of honor decreed that they must kill themselves too. One after another, they performed a gruesome ritual suicide, slicing their stomachs open in disembowelment. But it was a mistake. The castle was not burning, and their lord was safe. One boy survived and revealed the truth. The story is often quoted as an inspiring example of samurai loyalty, or, on the other hand, to show how war wastes the lives of the young.

Next, we drove across a bridge over the river Shiokawa, which means salt, because it was once used to bring salt up the river from Niigata on the coast, and soon arrived in Kitakata, an old farming town famous for its *kuras,* or traditional storehouses. More than a hundred years ago, a fire swept through the village destroying everything except the storehouses. Since then the residents have copied the storehouse design for almost all the town buildings, using the traditional style of thick plaster walls, sloping tiled roofs, an ornate front door, and family crest placed just under the front peak of the roof. Some *kuras* have wood strips on yellow walls, some are made of brick, some have thick shutters painted white with black decoration.

In a field, two women weeded a bed of tall flowers. The older one gave a wide smile, and I saw her front teeth were blackened in the traditional fashion. She wore a large cotton kerchief tied around her head and neck, pale mauve overalls, and underneath a black sweater tucked into narrow dark blue pants. She looked very like the farm woman Isabella Bird saw with a "thoroughly good-natured face rendered hideous by black teeth, who wore straw sandals, blue cotton trousers with a vest tucked into them, and a blue cotton towel knotted round her head."

From here, Nina turned off into the mountains for Tajima. It was dark by the time we arrived. Her house, which had once been a temple, was a low building with wood floors and screens dividing the rooms. The walls and ceilings were painted white. The modern kitchen had a stove, refrigerator, double sink and a high table with stools round it.

Nina telephoned her neighbor, Kiki, a Japanese woman who was an expert in local history, whom Nina thought might know about Isabella Bird. Kiki arrived within minutes. Her dark hair was pulled back in a neat chignon. She had smooth creamy skin, a pair of tiny fashionable glasses on her perfectly shaped nose, and the assertive manner of one accustomed to taking charge. Over her neat black pants and black sweater, she wore a loose check shirt with the word "Bitch" carefully embroidered over the left pocket. My Japanese wasn't up to translating it, but I wondered if she knew what it meant. I'd noticed Japanese ads and signs as well as printing on jackets, caps, and tee-shirts using odd phrases in English, as if the letters themselves were decoration enough, and no one cared what they said.

Kiki opened the book she had brought with her. It was a history of Tajima, published a few years ago. She pointed to a familiar photograph of Isabella Bird, looking stout and matronly, and read as Nina translated about her life, childhood, and travels, in particular her visit to Japan and her stop in Tajima, which, the writer asserted, she always remembered fondly. In fact, Isabella Bird stopped briefly in Tajima to change horses and observed it was, "for a Japanese town, rather picturesque."

I showed Kiki my biography, and we talked about Bird's travels in Colorado, where I live, and her other journeys to China, Korea, Russia, and other exotic places. Kiki was most excited, so we invited her to come touring in Tajima the next day.

That night I slept in the main room on spotless mats, with three futons below and four quilts on top to keep me warm. The room had long windows that looked out on the distant mountain ranges. It was beautifully quiet and still, and I woke as the morning light filtered through the clouds.

When Isabella Bird rode through the area, she commented: "The country was really very beautiful. The views were wider and finer, taking in great sweeps of peaked mountains, wooded to their summits, and from the top of the Pass of Sanno the clustered peaks were glorified into unearthly beauty in a gold mist of evening sunshine." She stayed in "the hamlet of Ouchi, prettily situated in a valley with mountainous surroundings, and, leaving early on the following morning, she had a very grand ride passing the pretty little lake of Oyake, and then ascending the magnificent pass to Ichikawa."

In 1878, Ouchi was a flourishing post town on the main road that linked the north and the south, the only route for transportation and travel. After the Meiji Restoration in 1884, the road was moved east and replaced with National Highway 121. Ouchi became a ghost town and was forgotten.

In recent years, its historic houses have been rediscovered and restored, and it's now a popular tourist attraction called Ouchi-Juku. The approach is through the same mountainous countryside that Isabella Bird saw, though on a smooth tarmacadam road zigzagging round hairpin bends. The village's wide main street is lined with traditional white-washed thatched-roof houses, completely restored to look just as it did a century ago. A few houses have been restored inside so that you can see how people lived in the old days, with open pit fireplaces, kettles hanging from the ceilings, and plain wooden floors with cushions. Most of the other houses have modern interiors. People still live here and have to conform to preservation rules for the town.

There are also shops offering souvenirs, local specialties, and food. One window had a colorful display of gourds of different sizes, locally grown apples, and egg-size eggplants on branches for flower arrangements. In the hardware store, the walls and counters were covered with towels, whisks, spoons, measures, bowls, basins, table-cloths, rolled mats, little paper umbrellas, and dozens of souvenirs. Another store offered packets of colored paper in delicate shades of mauve and pink and yellow for origami. Next door was an art studio, with framed pictures on the wall and stacks of prints in boxes. On a stall in the open air were boxes of grasshoppers, paper umbrellas, wooden bowls and spoons, hanging cloths, cooking utensils, sake in various shaped bottles, toy animals, and books. A smell of barbecue filled the air from a grill on wheels where a surly man cooked tiny whole fish on sticks. Through the window behind him, I watched two people roll and pat dough to make rice cakes, or *mochi*, on a flat stone counter.

Kiki led us to a souvenir store she knew where she spoke briskly to the owner. We sat outside under the awning among displays of wigs, masks, kimonos, and other disguises for the annual July parade. In seconds, a slender woman wearing a thick coat over her long robe brought us a tray with cups of steaming hot buckwheat tea and *mochi* cakes. Kiki explained that this was a special occasion, and she was so happy to be here with us.

Nina picked up one of the rubber wigs and put it on. Shaped like the complicated black chignons of Japanese geishas and decorated with white ribbon, the wig transformed her, and she folded her hands in front of her and looked down demurely. I tried a wig on too, and then added one of the traditional cone-shaped straw hats, and Nina and I posed for photographs.

Nina told us that she had been invited to take part in the annual *matsuri,* or festival parade, a year ago, when she wore the mask and traditional Japanese robes.

"I was one of the few non-Japanese ever to take part in the parade, and I've never been more photographed in my life," Nina said. "It was a real honor. But you can only take part once in your lifetime, so I can never do it again."

Overlooking the street, an imposing shrine stood on top of the steep hill at the far end, a memorial to Prince Mochihito Takakura. He was the emperor's son who fled from the south in 1868 to escape his attackers and died here, as did his wife, Princess Sakuragi. I wondered if Isabella Bird had walked up to the shrine and the adjoining cemetery, now overgrown with weeds and grasses, and looked at the headstones on the steep slope.

Below the bluff where the temple stood was a bird's-eye view of the historic road lined with old houses. I looked down at the people strolling along, taking photographs, and talking to each other. Among the raincoats and umbrellas, I suddenly noticed two women in traditional Japanese dress. The bright gleam of their pink and yellow long silken robes, wide belts round their waists, white socks, and thick heavy shoes on their feet, were a startling contrast to the drabness of the gray day. They sheltered from the rain under a shiny pink umbrella and hurried along the gleaming wet roadway to one of the houses.

From the village of Ouchi, Isabella Bird's route lay northwest. She took the main road, "a villainous track, with depressions more than a foot deep formed by the treading of the pack-horses in each other's footsteps. Each hole was a quagmire of tenacious mud, and the leader adjured the animals the whole time with 'Hai! Hai! Hai!' which is supposed to suggest to them that extreme caution is requisite." She added wearily: "Good roads are really the most pressing need of Japan."

I left Ouchi driving along smooth roads that whisked me through the mountains, over a rushing river, past sloping hillsides of evergreen trees, to the Folklore Museum. On display were some of the old wooden saddles with padded seats and rope girths that Isabella Bird had used, as well as reins and halters. There were dozens of kitchen utensils, farming tools, woodworking implements, and a display of imposing wood ceremonial drums, carved wooden bowls, and fertility symbols of smooth shiny dark wood, shaped into giant penises and vaginas, showing the creativity of the old woodworkers. Another display showed silkworms, because silk was once a thriving home industry. People fed the silkworms mulberry leaves, watched them spin cocoons, reeled the silk from the cocoons, and wove cloth.

The museum director invited me into his office, which was filled with desks and closets and papers. A sad-faced man with a beige jacket over his shirt and tie, he served us hot, strong coffee as Nina explained what I was doing. At the mention of Isabella Bird's name, he leapt to his feet, went to a shelf, and came back with a copy of Isabella Bird's book in Japanese. He knew all about her!

His passion in life was researching the history of the old Tajima road and those who traveled along it. It used to be called Nishikaido. *Nishi* means west, and she took the road west. He brought out several weighty copies of a scholarly journal he edits and told me enthusiastically: "I have been studying the road for twenty years. I have written one book, and I have put together several papers and books of papers about the road. It was the route that people took through Tajima and I know it well." He made copies of one of his articles, handed me his card, and urged me to send him a copy of my book on Japan. He bowed, and we shook hands. Isabella Bird had found me another friend.

For Nina's lunch as my guide I asked her where she would like to eat. She said her favorite restaurant was called *The Bamboo*, run for the past thirteen years by a Japanese couple. I assumed it was a Japanese place and was eagerly looking forward to sushi and sashimi, perhaps with a delicious soup to start with, because it was late and I was hungry.

We drove for quite a while along winding roads. Finally, Nina turned the car into a shopping area and parked, and we walked up the stairs to the restaurant.

The Bamboo was a light airy place with big windows looking over the rain-soaked mountains. Nina was warmly welcomed by the owners, a friendly attractive young couple, and we sat at a table in the window. We were the only customers. I picked up the menu, and realized that this was an Italian restaurant.

The menu offered café au lait, creme café au lait, coffee float, freshly squeezed juice, tea, cola, yogurt, ice cream, crêpes, and parfaits. There were Bamboo Original Drinks such as Bananacho, which was banana juice and chocolate, and Maccha au Lait—green tea and milk. For lunch there was tuna on toast, bean paste on toast, vegetable sandwich, mushroom curry, hamburg (with or without cheese) with Japanese Style sauce, spaghetti Neopolitan, Mentaiko, Tuna, and Yaki, and Hamburg Cream Spaghetti.

Nina ordered her favorite dish—spaghetti with mushrooms and cream sauce. I asked for spaghetti in cream sauce with shrimp and mushrooms. We had fresh Parmesan cheese. It was absolutely delicious and would have won awards in any country. We ordered dessert—Nina had a chocolate parfait, which had three scoops of ice cream with whipped cream, a cherry, and chocolate sauce, and I chose *setto*, a slice of light sweet cheesecake with a little red raspberry sauce and whipped cream. The *cappucino* was excellent, too, though it was a little strange ordering it in Japanese.

Nina rushed me to the nearest local station to catch the train to my next stop. I peered out through the rain-spattered windows feeling relaxed, well-fed, warm, and dry, and murmured *Arrividerci* as I watched her car speed down the mountain road.

Chapter 4
Discovering
Yamagata

Yamagata prefecture impresses me as being singularly prosperous, progressive and go-ahead; the plain of Yamagata, which I entered soon after leaving Kaminoyama, is populous and highly cultivated, and the broad road, with its enormous traffic, looks wealthy and civilized. I was delighted to come upon the only thoroughly solid piece of modern Japanese work I have met with—a remarkably handsome stone bridge—the first I have seen.

Isabella Bird, 1878

The countryside will recall scenes from Japanese woodblock prints, with farm houses, rice fields, drying persimmons. Castle towns will satisfy any desire for the conveniences of city life with hotels and inns, department stores, museums, antique shops. Since Tohuku is Japan's main rice-producing area, the fine quality of the rice makes superb sake. Other food specialties include various fish, fruits, vegetables, and buckwheat noodles. It is still the unspoiled part of the country.

Tourist brochure, 1998

T he old grandfather clock outside in the hall strikes eight o'clock. I am alone in my room in a *ryokan*, an old-fashioned Japanese hot springs inn, in the mountains of Yamagata.

My room on the second floor of the old inn has smooth tatami mats. A low table sits in the middle, with a thermos of hot water and a tray with cups and a bowl for tea. On the floor are deep pink cushions with a white design of swirling circles. Simple white curtains hang at the low windows which are covered with traditional rice-paper *shoji* screens. I slide back the screens and open one of the windows. I can hear the rain thudding and splashing on the straw roof above me. It's heavy dark outside, no lights anywhere, hot and humid. Dark clouds warn of the typhoon blowing north which, according to the weather reports, is scheduled to arrive soon. The rain drowns the sounds of the traffic on the highway.

The futon lies unrolled on the floor by the wall farthest from the door. There's a small hard square pillow and a mound of tempting quilts. Above, hanging precariously from the ceiling, is a bulky metal heater, reminding me that people stay here in the winter to ski. A big wooden closet sits against the wall. I open the heavy drawers and find pillows and blankets. On top of a low antique bureau of dark wood is a square metal safe with a key, a TV with a slot for 100 yen coins, and an oblong mirror in a frame. Everything is clean and shiny in a charming old-fashioned way, and there's a pleasant smell of flowers.

Isabella Bird used the phrase "no purposeless bothers" to describe the happy freedom she felt when she traveled. It was a phrase that resonated with me. When I travel, there are "no purposeless bothers." Once I set off, and arrive somewhere I have never been before, I only have to think about traveling. I have the exhilarating feeling that all things are possible, and I can begin afresh discovering an unknown place. I welcome the journey to be experienced as it unfolds. I may lose my tickets, or miss the bus, or eat a terrible meal, or find the hotel never received my reservation, or arrive at the world's best museum and find it closed for the season, or visit a magnificent view to discover it's covered in impenetrable mist, but that's just part of the fabric of travel. The good things and the bad things make up the sum of the experience. Every traveler finds her own experiences and sees her journey through a prism of individuality.

I arrived by train in Yamagata this morning. The Yamagata prefecture in the Tohuku region now stretches from Yonezawa in the south to Shinjo in the north. Yamagata City, the prefectural capital, with a population of more than 250,000, is situated between the two towns and is about an hour by train north of Aizu-Wakamatsu.

After I walked around the station for anxious minutes wondering if my guide would materialize, an earnest young man with glasses and thick black hair came up to me and asked: "Eberren Kaye?" I said, "Oh yes!" with relief, quite forgetting the polite phrases of welcome I'd been practicing in Japanese. Mr. Kaito, a friendly, energetic young man, wore a white shirt and blue jeans with a brown leather belt. He was from the regional tourist office, would drive me to Shinjo for lunch to meet my guide and translator, and we would all go to Kaneyama to see a memorial to Isabella Bird.

His Honda, very like the one I drive in Colorado, zipped along the smooth highways. Mr. Kaito knew a good deal of English but was embarrassed about speaking it, like many Japanese people I met. Using my dictionary and our mutual determination to communicate, we managed to talk. To my amazement, he was yet another person who knew all about Isabella Bird and had read her book, translated into Japanese.

He told me that in 1985 Yamagata officials developed a program with the imposing title of the Seventh General Development Plan of Yamagata Prefecture to beautify, preserve, and improve the region's environment. They decided to call it the Arcadia Plan, taking the phrase from Bird's comment in her book about the region resembling "an

Asiatic Arcadia." The Arcadia Plan was widely promoted for ten years, so Bird's name and book are now well-known.

Isabella Bird praised the entire Yamagata region and wrote: "The plain of Yonezawa, with the prosperous town of Yonezawa in the south, and the frequented watering-place of Akayu in the north, is a perfect garden of Eden, a smiling and plenteous land, an 'Asiatic Arcadia,' prosperous and independent, all its bounteous acres belonging to those who cultivate them, who live under their vines, figs, and pomegranates, free from oppression."

Mr. Kaito also quite understood why I would want to follow Bird's footsteps. In Japan more than 300 years ago, the renowned Japanese poet Basho went on a pilgrimage through northern Japan, which he said "might as well be going to the ends of the earth." Today, the Japanese often follow his route and those of other famous writers and travelers on their own pilgrimages.

As we drove into Shinjo, I remembered Isabella Bird's caustic description: "Shinjo is a wretched place. It has an air of decay. It is a wretched town of over 5,000 people, situated in a plain of rice-fields. Shinjo has a large trade in rice, silk, and hemp, and ought not to be as poor as it looks. The mosquitoes were in their thousands, and I had to go to bed, so as to be out of their reach, before I had finished my wretched meal of sago and condensed milk. There was a hot rain all night, my wretched room was dirty and stifling, and rats gnawed my boots and ran away with my cucumbers."

Today, Shinjo is a bustling business town with traffic, cars jockeying for parking places, bicycles, buses, taxis, restaurants, stores, office buildings, and people walking purposefully along the streets. It's renowned for its famous buckwheat noodles, *soba*, made with fresh mountain water. After Mr. Kaito parked his car, we walked to the best noodle restaurant in town.

The entrance doorway opened into one room filled with people. There was a steady buzz of conversation from business men—and a few women—sitting on cushions around low tables. I was the only foreigner. I followed Mr. Kaito to the far end of the room and, after taking off my shoes, sat down on a cushion on the low bench. Waiting for us was my guide, another Mr. Ito, who eagerly shook my hand. He was a retired high school English teacher and spoke English clearly and fluently. An exuberant, cheerful man, with tousled black hair, a lively expression, and a ready smile, he could hardly wait to tell me that Ito was the name of Miss Bird's assistant too, though he said it was a very common Japanese name. He had just read Bird's book aloud in Japanese to his wife and his mother, and they had all enjoyed it.

Our server, a short gray-haired woman with a fierce expression, immediately brought us a cup of green tea to drink. It was delicious. I smiled at the serving lady, and gestured for some more tea. Her face flushed, she looked outraged and erupted into excited Japanese. Mr. Kaito and Mr. Ito looked very embarrassed, conferred briefly, and told me I couldn't have any more tea because the restaurant only serves one cup. After that, you drink the *soba* water in which the noodles are cooked. I was quite mortified. It was clear I had committed a serious error of Japanese etiquette, and I apologized profusely. The server plunked down two large kettles of soba water. Mr. Kaito quickly poured me a cup. It tasted like the salty water that noodles were cooked in, but I said it was delicious.

Bowls of noodles arrived accompanied by a pickle, mustard and onions, and a small dipping bowl for the sauce. The noodles tasted excellent, though tricky to manage with chopsticks, which I was determined to use correctly to atone for my previous social slip.

Afterwards, we walked back to the car. The air was hot and humid. A typhoon had hit southern Japan the previous day and was sweeping north with fierce winds and heavy rains. On the horizon, looming over the rooftops and distant mountains, were thick gray, black, and white clouds, hovering in a wide threatening circle. Above us, the sun poured down from a cloudless bright blue sky. We were in the eye of the typhoon, the calm center before the storm was predicted to arrive later that day.

We left Shinjo for Kaneyama, following Isabella Bird's route northeast through the mountains. The highway led up hills with forests of evergreen trees on either side, through small towns and sprawling farm lands. As we drove into the town of Kaneyama, Mr. Kaito took winding narrow streets to an elementary school, a modern three-story brick building lined with windows, which was closed because it was Sunday. He pulled into the parking lot.

As I got out of the car, a local official hurried over to welcome me and introduced a reporter from the newspaper. They bowed politely, and we all exchanged cards. I was surprised to realize that my visit was worthy of such special attention. After more introductions, I followed the local official across the parking lot, with Mr. Kaito and Mr. Ito behind. I had no idea what the memorial would be like and imagined a plaque on the building or a sign explaining that Isabella Bird had stayed here for a couple of days resting before setting off north.

The official stopped and pointed in front of him. I looked in astonishment. On a raised concrete platform surrounded by green grass was a huge, stunning and impressive black shiny cube ornamented with wide strips of stainless steel. It was like a memorial to a national celebrity, with a futuristic *Star Wars* feeling. I gawped at it, speechless, unable to imagine why such a significant creation had been erected to honor Isabella Bird in this town in Japan.

I walked round it, admiring the inscriptions. Beautifully carved on the front in Japanese and English was the paragraph that Isabella Bird wrote about her brief and pleasant stay in Kaneyama. On the back of the cube was another engraved paragraph in Japanese from the Kaneyama Town Council, which Mr. Ito translated:

"The British born Isabella Bird (1831-1904), came to Japan and visited the far north area. She had many difficulties along the way. On her way, she passed through Kaneyama, and admired the beautiful nature, and found the people very kind and warm. She liked it here and stayed here with a peaceful mind a hundred years ago. We decided to make this memorial. Kaneyama Town. November 1988."

Mr. Ito explained that many people had read Bird's book, and asserted, "Every child in school knows her book and every citizen knows her name!"

The monument, designed by Professor Haruhiko Yasuda of Musashino Fine Arts University, had cost 2.5 million yen to design and erect. A solid cube about three feet on each side, it's made of Indian black granite, with stainless steel on the front and rear. Kaneyama Town Council organized a special unveiling ceremony in November 1988, which some 70 guests attended including Professor Kenkichi Takanashi, who translated Bird's book into Japanese.

I was astonished at this splendid recognition of Isabella Bird's visit and at the excitement that I had generated by coming to see it. I photographed the monument. Mr. Kaito photographed me at the monument. Mr. Ito photographed me at the monument with my camera. The reporter photographed the official and me at the monument and then interviewed me about why I had come to see it.

Next, we toured Kaneyama's newly restored old town, which looks much as it did a century ago. The historic stone canals and ditches that wind through the narrow streets have been rebuilt with new wooden bridges and beds of flowers along the canal banks. Fat golden *koi* or carp swim about lazily in the water. A family with two little girls were laughing as they threw crumbs into the water and the glittering fish splashed for them.

Many of the old houses are made of red cedar wood, for which the town is famous, and some of the red cedar trees are more than 200 years old The houses are painted white with designs of oblongs and squares in black, and big windows. They looked like the storehouses I saw in Kitakata. Home owners receive a bonus from the local council to restore the historic homes by using stone foundations and thatched roofs, and to rebuild the upper floors in traditional style with plaster and wood. We were just leaving when I noticed a store on the main street had a sign hanging outside in English: "Isabera Construction Company." Isabella Bird would have enjoyed that!

Mr. Kaito drove me through the mountains to a traditional Japanese hot springs mountain inn, a picture-perfect thatched roof house, sheltered by trees and bushes and nestled against the hillside. Just beyond the formal garden is a lake with tall reeds. The sun was sinking behind the mountains to the west, tinting the trees and shrubs and lake a delicate pinky-orange from the reflected light.

The young woman who greeted us stared at me in surprise. She told Mr. Kaito that she thought I was going to be a man! After we'd agreed that I was definitely female and staying on my own, she led me along the wooden floors of a narrow corridor with doors on one side. The wooden floors felt uneven and squeaked here and there.

She pulled back the sliding *shoji* screen to my room, I took off my slippers and went in. A low window let in the late afternoon sunshine. On the floor were spotless tatami mats, a low table, cushions, and a rolled-out futon. I followed her out of the room—slippers on—and walked behind her along another corridor to the toilet—slippers off—and the two wash basins. The hot springs bathroom was downstairs near the entrance lobby.

Back in my room, I lay down on the futon. I decided I would take a hot bath, wait for dinner in my room at six, and go to bed early. I picked up the dark blue and white cotton robe neatly folded on the bed.

On the rail was the traditional small square towel. I put on my slippers and walked down to the hot springs bath room.

Several of my guidebooks explained the proper etiquette for a Japanese bath, so I knew what to do. First I had to undress, then wash myself with soap and rinse it off thoroughly, and then I could get into the steaming hot bath.

I had the place entirely to myself. I undressed in the outside room, putting my clothes and slippers into the basket on the shelf, and put the folded robe on top. Taking the square of towel, I opened the heavy door into the steamy bath room. It was warm, humid, misty, and relaxing. I sat down at one of the stools facing a row of vanity mirrors, hand showers attached to the sinks, and a counter lined with a selection of plastic containers with squirt tops, all labeled in Japanese with different designs and colors. I guessed they were soap, shampoo, conditioner, body lotions, and creams. But which was which? My dictionary was in my room, and I would have had a hard time matching the Japanese squiggles with the neat print on the page. I picked up a yellow bottle and sniffed it. It smelled very sweet and strong. I picked up a pink container and squirted some pink foamy liquid into my hand. It looked like soap, so I washed myself all over with it. The soap smelled wonderful, very rich and fruity. I rinsed off carefully with the handheld shower, from my head down my shoulders and back, and even stood up to rinse off my legs, though you are supposed to be able to wash sitting down.

I needed to wash my hair. I chose a fancy egg-timer shaped white container with a wavy design and squirted white liquid onto my wet hair. It made a great lather and smelled of almonds. I carefully rinsed off the shampoo with the handheld shower. Now I was clean. Leaving my towel on the stool, I went over to the tub and put my foot in. The water was steaming hot, but not unbearable. I sat on the edge with my feet in, then stood up in it—the water reached to just above my knees— and then eased myself into the hot water, floating in the relaxing warmth. The bath was painted a deep blue so the water was a beautiful color. I leaned back against the edge, my arms along the side, and looked up at the dark squares of steam-covered windows.

There was a wonderful sense of freedom, to be naked, clean, and completely alone in the hot bath, somewhere in Japan. I got out a couple of times and sat on the edge, cooling down, and then slipped into the water again to float weightlessly, breathing in the warm steam, relaxing into total apathy. I had a sense of timelessness, of being part of the history of women floating in warm water, from geisha to globetrotter. I wondered how Isabella Bird managed in her hot springs bath in her inn and if she too thought about being part of history, or if she was more concerned with easing her aching back.

After about half an hour, my fingers were as wrinkled as crepe paper. I climbed out and dried myself off with the tiny towel, wringing it out as I'd been told. This is the traditional way to dry off, and it does work, but I'd prefer a large, thick American towel any day. Isabella Bird felt the same: "The benefit of these and other medicinal waters would be much increased if vigorous friction replaced the dabbing with soft towels," she wrote crisply.

I walked out to the dressing room, wrapped the blue robe around me and tied the belt, put the slippers on, picked up my clothes, and flip-flopped back to my room. I felt relaxed, warm, safe, and happy.

There was a knock at the door. My hostess brought in a big wooden tray, which she put it on the table. She knelt down beside it and gestured for me to sit on a cushion beside her, so she could explain what she had made for dinner. The tray had about a dozen individual china and lacquer bowls and dishes, which presented an appealing pattern of color and design, from the green of the roots against the small white bowl to the earthenware casserole with the *kuri*. At first, I thought that meant curry but using my dictionary and her signs, I found out they were chestnuts, from the nearby mountains. The dinner menu was:

A rice cooker with rice

Mountain mushroom and fish soup

A plate of *koi* or carp in a sweet caramel sauce

Thin slices of raw fish with a kind of soy sauce to dip them in

A few pieces of lily roots in a sweet sauce

Kuri gohan, a casserole with rice and sliced chestnuts from the
mountains

Soba noodles with seaweed, or *nuri*

A dish of green vegetables, sliced into small pieces

A dish of mushrooms

Nimono, a dish of potatoes, stewed beef strips, and tofu squares

Bowl of soy sauce

A persimmon with its peel almost off, cut into four pieces, like a
flower in the bowl

The beer came in a can and water in a glass. She bowed and left. I tried everything. The fish soup was spicy and refreshing. The sweet caramel sauce made the koi taste almost like a dessert. I loved the lily roots and raw fish, savoring the different textures and tastes. I tasted the *kuri* but it had an odd slightly bitter flavor. I did appreciate it as a local delicacy, but I didn't have the local taste for it. The vegetables and potato stew were wonderful and full of subtle spices. I could not finish the *soba* and *nuri*. I ate the orange persimmon for dessert; it had a distinctive taste—not very sweet but juicy and refreshing.

I felt like royalty. The meal was so elegantly presented, so beautifully prepared, and so tasty, that I regretted coming to the end. It was completely relaxing to sit on a cushion, in a loose robe, eating tasty food on my own. I thought how much more civilized this was than trying to find a restaurant, decipher a Japanese menu, and eat at a table surrounded by other people.

As I sat there thinking about the meal, I heard a knock on the door. My hostess wanted to know how the meal was. With dictionary in hand, we talked about what I'd liked, and what I'd left. She smiled and bowed a lot, and took my tray away.

I imagine that if the inn were full of people, I would have heard talking in the other rooms, screens sliding open and shut, the rattle of bowls and cups, and footsteps in the creaky wooden corridors as the guests walked to the bathroom and back. Most guests come in the summer to walk in the mountains or in the winter to ski.

Even in her comfortable inn in Yamagata, Isabella Bird was besieged with biting insects. Her arm was swollen from bites by a hornet and a gadfly, and she lamented: "I am also suffering from the bites of horse ants, which attack one in walking. Besides these, there is a fly, as harmless in appearance our house-fly, which bites as badly as a mosquito."

It was dark. I could hear rain pouring down on the thatched roof overhead. The air was thick with wet heat. I curled up on the futon to read. Suddenly, something moving above caught my eye. Walking across the ceiling near the neon lights were large, long-legged black bugs. They crawled slowly across the ceiling, silhouetted perfectly against the white paint. A couple flapped their wings and dropped to the floor. I got up and eyed them, wondering if they would bite, and recognized the spiky legs, red marked bodies, and long antenna on their heads. They looked just like the box elder bugs, or stink bugs, that invade my kitchen every winter in Colorado. I know them well, and squish them frequently. They are mellow insects, quiet, slow-moving, short-sighted. They eat only box elder leaves, and have no enemies, because no other animal or bird eats them since they taste so bad. If annoyed, they emit a bad smell or fly at you with a humming buzz but do nothing else. I took a piece of paper, caught them expertly, squished firmly till I heard a soft crunch, and dropped them in the trash can.

It was silly to worry about such harmless insects, I realized, or even the solitary mosquito I could hear buzzing around. I closed the windows, turned off the light, put my head on the hard pillow, and fell asleep.

Chapter 5
Nanyo and
Kawanishi

Mr. Brunton's excellent map fails in this region, so it is only by fixing on the well-known city of Yamagata and devising routes to it that we get on. Half the evening is spent consulting Japanese maps, if we can get them, and in questioning the house-master and Transport Agent, and any chance travelers.

Isabella Bird in Yamagata,
1878

Situated in southern Tohuku, Yamagata is shaped like a face. New transportation links such as the Yamagata Shinkansen, the Tokyo Expressway, in addition to Yamagata Airport make it possible to reach many points in Japan quickly and conveniently. Yamagata City is only 30 minutes by car from the airport, and is close to the hot springs cities of Tendo and Kaminoyama.

Tourist booklet with detailed
maps of Yamagata province,
1998

Traveling north on the road to Nanyo, Isabella Bird described it as "one of the great routes of Japanese travel, and it is interesting to see watering-places with their habits, amusements, and civilization quite complete, but borrowing nothing from Europe." She planned to stay overnight at a hot springs resort and enjoy the sulphur springs, but "it was one of the noisiest places I have seen. In the most crowded part, there are bathing sheds which were full of people of both sexes, splashing loudly, and the hubbub was unbearable."

I traveled along the road to visit Nanyo's Hygeia Park Community Center. Named after Hygeia, the Greek goddess of health, the recently built facility provides hot springs baths, swimming, exercise classes, and other activities for local residents. When I arrived in the morning, a cheerful but decorous group of senior citizens was filing into the center from their bus to spend the day. Outside the building, smooth green lawns stretched up a slope to a row of small huts that people who spent the day there could rent.

The director welcomed me in the lobby as I took off my shoes. We exchanged cards, bowed, and shook hands. He was a solid, well-built man with thick short dark hair, a quiet voice, and, in his dark suit and tie, looked a bit like Alfred Hitchcock. He was eager to show me the center. We began with the spacious first floor display area. I followed him to the rear of the lobby and could hardly believe my eyes.

The entire length of the back wall was lined with tall glass display cases, brightly lit. Inside was everything you would ever want to know about Isabella Bird! An outsize map of Japan had 28 blue dots marking the places she had visited on her journey to the north. Next to it was a large map of the world marking every place she had visited in her lifetime. Pinned up were photos, letters, and quotations about her travels, including comments from the 1878 English community in Japan including Ernest Satow (1842-1929), Basil Hall Chamberlain (1850-1935), Harry Smith Parkes (1843-1929), and James Curtis Hepburn (1815-1911), who was the first person to use Roman letters to interpret the Japanese language.

I walked along reading the English descriptions. Her books were all displayed in a line with their original covers. On one wall was a photograph of Isabella Bird on her wedding day in 1881, when she determinedly wore black to show she was still in mourning for her beloved sister, who had died the year before. There were also drawings and pictures from her books on Tibet, Persia, and Korea. An original letter in her spidery handwriting sent from Japan to her publisher, John Murray in London, apologized for not sending him some information sooner.

In front of the wall displays stood a separate well-lit glass case, about five feet high, with a large mounted photograph of Isabella Bird in her later years. The photo was set on a pedestal with a spotlight shining on it and had a printed sign with information about her. I looked at the display absolutely stunned to find such an extensive memorial.

In a separate glass case were artifacts of nineteenth century traveling gear—a steamer trunk, a black dress, a pith helmet, and a telescope. Isabella Bird wrote in her Japan book that she decided not to wear a pith helmet because she preferred the Japanese straw, cone-shaped hat. I asked the director where these items had come from. He nodded his head diplomatically: "A few people on the Arcadia Committee knew about Isabella Bird. When we decided to erect a memorial to her because she passed through here, two of the committee members went to England to see where she was born, and brought back these things." He smiled: "We don't know if these are really hers or not."

Afterwards, as we sat over coffee at a table in an upstairs cafeteria that overlooked the sweep of mountains surrounding the area, he handed me a leaflet in Japanese with a copy of one of her photographs on it.

"We are going to have an Isabella Bird photo contest this year for the first time," he explained. "Any photograph of the region she saw that shows nature, culture, festival, or historical aspects can be submitted, and the winners will be displayed in the Isabella Bird corner. Several prizes will be awarded."

I told him how thrilled Isabella Bird would have been to hear about the contest. She discovered photography while traveling through Persia a few years after her Japan trip, and later took photography classes in London. In China, she carried a heavy tripod camera with her and developed and printed her photos as she traveled.

The director urged me to have lunch in the dining room downstairs, though he would be unable to join us. It was a pleasant open room with about 30 plain wooden tables and chairs. A special soup of the region, *enomi*, was on the menu. Mr. Ito and I sat at a table by big windows that looked out on a circle of green trees.

A young woman served us each a large bowl of soup. *Enomi* had slices of beef, squares of a sort of gelatinous tofu, the famous Yamagata *taro* potatoes, which are essential to the dish, spring onions, soy and water. It was like a tasty minestrone soup and very salty, and I asked for a glass of water, having looked the word up in my dictionary. Mr. Ito politely pointed out that I was using the wrong word. If you want a glass of water in a restaurant, you ask for *okia*, not *misu*, which is a general word for water. I thanked him and thought that a teacher is always a teacher!

He proved to be an excellent guide to Yamagata. He was full of all kinds of information which he shared at every opportunity. He loved to talk, had a good sense of humor, and was always cheerful and entertaining. His English was very easy to understand, and he had an extensive vocabulary. At one point, he took me aside to warn me that "some of the things I have told you may not be quite accurate, so please check them carefully." I assured him I would.

We left Nanyo to see Komatsu, which was a village where Isabella Bird stayed for one night in an inn, and where throngs of people stared at her. Today, Komatsu is a depressing-looking town with narrow streets and dingy stores. The corner of the main street where the inn used to stand is now a two-pump Shell gas station. The road still follows the same route and a side street beside the gas station leads to a bridge that Isabella Bird crossed on her way to the inn.

I walked from the gas station round a bend to cross over the rushing stream on the bridge. I looked upstream where the water was confined to a narrow canal running between the road and the back gardens of houses along the street, edged with low stone walls. Flowers, rows of vegetables, and green lawns filled the gardens. Downstream, the canal curved round a corner and disappeared into a mess of overgrown bushes. The unpainted walls of warehouses and car repair shops lined the street. It was very different from what she had described.

The next stop was Kawanishi, a farm town with narrow streets, thick green hedges, and open fields. We turned off at the Archaeological Museum, a low building set back from the road. Crowded inside were shelves and glass cases with a motley collection of geological specimens, including an unexpected photograph of Isabella Bird in her black dress, with a sign about her 1878 visit. I hadn't thought of her as a geological specimen before.

Outside the museum, there was a more significant reminder. As part of the Arcadia Campaign, a twelve-foot high wrought iron arch had been erected to symbolize unity among towns and villages that wanted to preserve the region. Silhouetted against the sky, the arch was decorated with carved flowers, flying birds, curling stems, and a shining sun. In front stood a large solid rock with a plaque embedded in its surface. Once again I read Isabella Bird's quotation about the beautiful plain of Yonezawa, with the date, to commemorate her 1878 visit.

I knew that Isabella Bird loved flowers as she traveled, though in Japan she described mostly the greenery she passed with only mentions of a few flowers such as wisteria, azaleas, hydrangeas, and the yellow Japan lily. In October, Kawanishi holds a nationally renowned dahlia festival for a few weeks when the dahlias are in full bloom. I knew that this was one event Isabella Bird would not have missed, so I went to see it.

A rolling sea of colorful flowers set out in rectangular, semicircular, and round beds filled a sunken area the size of a football field. Thousands of blooming dahlias in every color under the sun waved in the breeze. It was an cornucopia of red and pink and orange and crimson and mauve and white and yellow and cream and scarlet flowers, in dozens of shapes, sizes, and heights. Wide stone steps led down to the flower beds, and paths led between them. I saw dahlias with long wispy petals, thick layered petals, tiny pointed petals, large fat petals. Some plants stood tall in the air, others grew low to the ground, others clumped together at mid-height. Some blossomed from plants thick with leaves, while others burst into flower from long bare stems. Each one had a sign in Japanese with its name—"Sunny Smile" and

"Princess Matsuko" and "Evening Star"—and even a large purple one called Evelyn!

One stunning, deep red flower had white tips on the ends of its petals, as if brushed in snow. Another bursting into vivid orange and red looked as if it might catch fire. A soft red flower had a deep yellow center. Another had layer upon layer of fat sun-yellow petals. One plant had flowers of the softest, palest, most delicate shade of pink, like the inside of a seashell. As I walked along, the blossoms seemed to glow under the overcast gray skies. I was intoxicated by the brilliance of the colors and the sheer quantity of blossoms.

Mr. Ito told me that he and his wife liked to visit this show every year, and said;"It's not good to see this alone. You need to share the experience."

I felt a wave of nostalgia for my husband at home with my family, thinking what fun it would have been to stroll round this glorious floral display with him, and remembering beautiful gardens we had visited together in Pennsylvania and Alabama, New York and New Jersey, Hawaii, London, Edinburgh, and many other places. The times I most miss my husband on my travels are when I find something absolutely wonderful and desperately want to share it with him so he can enjoy it too. When I'm miserable or things go wrong, it's easier to be alone.

I sat down on a stone seat by a round table and bought a can of hot coffee from a vending machine, one of Japan's convenient automated services. On a pond nearby, colorful mallard ducks loudly quacked at almost-grown brown ducklings while two elegant aloof white swans paddled round the side, keeping away from the noise. A light drizzle fell, rippling the surface of the water.

It was time to go north to Yamagata City. The route still passes much of the same scenery that Isabella Bird saw. She found "an enchanting region of beauty, industry, and comfort, mountain girdled, and watered by the bright Matsuka. Everywhere there are prosperous and beautiful farming villages, with large houses with carved beams and ponderous tiled roofs, each standing its own grounds, buried among persimmons and pomegranates, with flower-gardens under trellised vines, and privacy secured by high, closely-clipped screen of pomegranate or cryptomeria."

On all sides I saw beautifully cultivated rolling fields with fruit trees and grape vines on trellises. The distant snow-topped mountains stood in a circle round the vast flat plain. The sun was sinking behind the peaks, tinting the clouds deep pink and soft gray. Across the valley, I saw fields with rice drying on wooden rails, bright green fields of new rice growing, which is planted here and there in the fall, apple trees heavy with red fruit, the bright orange of persimmons, and neat farmhouses tucked into sheltered nooks.

That evening, Mr. Kaito invited me to dinner with Mr. Tomo from the tourist office and two women who worked with them. We went to a Japanese restaurant that specialized in *oden*, a kind of stew with potatoes and a hard-boiled egg, squares of jelly-like tofu, meatballs on a skewer, vegetables, and liquid. On the table were bowls with squid, salad, pickles, spicy yellow mustard, and—my favorite—*umeboshi* or pickled plums. Asahi beer flowed freely, and we kept refilling our little beer glasses. It was a lively evening!

Mr. Tomo was a wiry, energetic man with a flat, calm-looking face. He wore glasses, spoke extremely quickly, and was used to being in charge. He knew a great deal about Isabella Bird's life, and it was a delight to talk to someone who knew almost as much about her as I did. The two women did most of the translating while Mr. Kaito chipped in every now and then. As his face became flushed from the beer, his English improved immensely!

Mr. Tomo had been one of the first people involved in the Arcadia Campaign, and wanted to know how I became interested in Isabella Bird. He had no idea she was so well known in Colorado and was surprised to hear there were no memorials to her there. He wondered why she didn't spend more time in Yamagata instead of Hokkaido, so we talked about that.

He knew that she had seen the old government buildings and he was eager to show me the new government buildings rebuilt on the same site, where he has an office. I followed the others out into the cool, damp evening. We walked down the street talking and joking, and turned the corner.

The modern Prefectural Building, newly cleaned and renovated, was bathed in floodlights. Two large towers stood on either side of the entrance, with a clock tower above the central facade. The stone balcony on the second floor looked as if it had been designed for politicians to address crowds assembled in the paved plaza below.

When Isabella Bird visited, the population was only 21,000 people, compared to more than 250,000 today. Describing the view from the main road, she wrote that "the Government Buildings, though in the usual confectionery style, are improved by the addition of verandahs, and the Court House, the Normal School, and the police buildings, are all in keeping with the good road and obvious prosperity. A large two-storied hospital, with a cupola, is nearly finished."

Mr. Tomo showed me an 1870s engraving. The old road stretched wide and straight away from the government buildings, but there were no vehicles on it, only people walking along carrying umbrellas and packages. I recognized the large buildings that Isabella Bird had seen and spotted the one with the cupola on top. Sadly, everything had been destroyed in a massive fire.

I turned to look at the wide, straight avenue that was now a modern road. The noise of the traffic had been a constant background as we stood talking. The road was filled with light from street lamps and the red tail lights and white head lights of traffic streaming up and down. On either side, tall offices loomed where once the old buildings had stood. But it was still the same road in the same place.

It was time to go. We took photographs of each other and of the government buildings. Standing on the sidewalk, talking and laughing, I was reluctant to end such a pleasant evening. We had been brought together by Isabella Bird who found Yamagata "progressive, go-ahead, highly cultivated, wealthy and civilized," which was high praise from her. I too had thoroughly enjoyed my visit here, the memorials I had discovered, the places I had seen, and the people I met who knew her.

I had to admit that I was sad at the thought that tomorrow morning I would catch a train and set off for a new place and another guide. I realized that, for me, the hardest part about traveling is not the difficulties that may arise, but having to say goodbye to people you like and may never see again.

Chapter 6
Lake
Tazawa and
Kakunodate

"Only strong people should travel in northern Japan. I have been suffering so much from my spine that I have been unable to travel more than seven or eight miles daily for several days, and even that with great difficulty. For six days and five nights the rain has never ceased, except for a few hours at a time, and for the last thirteen hours, it has been falling in such sheets as I have only seen for a few minutes at a time on the equator.

Isabella Bird, Tohuku, 1878

"Tohuku is where the traditional life of Japan is best preserved today. Its castle towns are among the most charming, its crafts are the earthiest, and its festivals are the lustiest. Still strongly rural, its people are plain-spoken and warm characters who retain vivid memories of the hardships that faced Tohuku farmers until only a few decades ago."

Gateway to Japan, June Kinoshita & Nicholas Palevsky, Kodansha International, 1998

A fearsome, fire-breathing dragon with flashing lights and smoke belching from its wide open mouth lurched onto the stage. Two cowering fishermen clutched each other in terror at the front; the music reached a crescendo with drums beating. The spotlight focused on the beautiful young woman in a floating white robe who sat on the dragon's head and began to sing.

I was at Waribi-za Arts Center theater watching a professional acting troupe in a play about the creation of Lake Tazawa, the deepest lake in Japan, which I had visited that morning. Legend says that Takko Hime, a young girl who wished to stay beautiful forever, prayed on a mountaintop for a hundred days, drank some water, and was transformed into a water dragon, with Lake Tazawa as her home. Hachitaro, a young man from a village, ate a magic fish and was also turned into a water dragon and forced to live in a nearby lagoon. The two met and fell in love, but a wicked sorcerer saw the young woman and also fell in love. The young man and the sorcerer fought, the young man was victorious, and married the young woman. Now, every year in the winter months, the young man leaves his lagoon to stay with his beloved in Lake Tazawa, and the passion of the two lovers heats up the water so much that it never freezes over.

The musical play provided plenty of action before the lovers were united at the end. It reminded me of an English pantomime with slapstick jokes, incredible stage effects, and lots of music and singing. Even though I couldn't understand the dialogue, the performance was lively and entertaining.

Lake Tazawa is a crater lake more than 1,300 feet deep, surrounded by forested hills. On the damp, windy fall morning when I visited, the water was gray, and it was hard to see even a few inches below the rippled surface. The tour boats that chug across the lake to see the statue of Takko Hime on the far western shore had canceled all trips after the people in one group came back seasick! Around the lake, the area has been developed into a popular summer tourist resort, with hotels and cottages, restaurants and souvenir shops, swan-shaped paddle boats, bicycle and hiking trails, a boardwalk, and a wide strip of sandy beach.

A bus ride away is the Arts Center, which has the theater, displays of pottery and paintings, a conference center and hotel, and a beer hall and cafeteria. I had lunch there and chose a delicious Japanese pizza with a very thin crust, mozzarella cheese, and round sliced tomatoes on top, washed down with apple juice.

Isabella Bird found little to eat—"I have been living here on rice, cucumbers, and salt salmon so salty that even after being boiled in two waters, it produces a most distressing thirst." One evening she had an omelette for dinner but never found any more eggs.

She had been traveling for three months, since leaving Tokyo in June, and she was exhausted. The weather was terrible, with torrential rain every day, and she confessed: "I suffered severely from pain and exhaustion, and almost fell into deep despair about ever reaching the sea."

When she reached an inn, she would desperately try to dry her soaked clothes before setting off the next morning. She was too tired to explore. She rode past "a village of samurai on a beautiful slope, with its fine detached houses, pretty gardens, deep-roofed gateways, grass and stone-faced terraces, and a look of refined, quiet comfort," but did not have the energy to stop.

In Kakunodate, a perfectly preserved street of samurai houses dates back to the time when the town was established in 1620. Of the original 80 samurai houses, the handful that remain today are considered among the best preserved examples of samurai architecture in Japan. From the railroad station, winding cobbled streets lead through the town to the street, which is shaded by tall weeping cherry trees brought from Kyoto more than 350 years ago. The 153 trees that remain are a National Natural Monument and are protected forever.

Originally built along a broad, central avenue, which led to the lord's hilltop castle, the houses stand today along a street lined with stone walls and dark wooden fences, wrought iron gates opening to stone paths that lead into low wooden houses, and gardens filled with tall green trees and shrubs. It was easy to imagine women in kimonos and traditional clogs clip-clopping along the street, rattling *kurama* carriages pulled by men over the cobbles, and the smell of smoke from open fireplaces.

The Ishiguro house is one of the oldest and dates back to 1809. It still has a thatched roof and two entrances—a main entrance for important visitors and a side entrance for family and servants. The family, who have been here since 1853, live in a newly built wing away from the tourists. The house has an open design with sliding paper screens dividing the inside area into separate rooms. The walls are plain with dark shiny wood panels or white paint, and there is little furniture or decoration. Spotless tatami mats edged with fabric cover the floors. Above the square pit fireplace lined with gray ashes, a black kettle hangs, suspended from the ceiling on a long bamboo stick.

A display of swords, a metal suit of armor, and long knives on the walls and in glass cases reminded me that the samurai were once the admired warriors of Japan. Several exquisite old Japanese robes, printed and woven on silk, hung on rods in the front room. One robe was made of flowing white silk with wide sleeves lined with red, decorated with delicate red flowers , blue-gray mountains, gray leaves, and yellow patterns woven together in a repetitive pattern. A second showed an abstract picture of fanciful white trees, white and yellow flowers, stark looming black clouds, and black mountains and sky sprinkled with moons and stars. The magnificent weaving looked as fresh as the day it was made, and the gleaming, colorful silk robes contrasted with the simplicity of the room.

A sliding door at the front of another house led to a covered wooden porch that overlooked a lush, green Japanese garden enclosed by a high, wooden fence. The only sounds were the drip of rain falling on leaves and the whoosh of passing cars on the wet road outside. The mottled trunk of an oak tree, reputed to be 250 years old, soared high into the air. A single black, smooth rock, gleaming in the rain, was carefully set in a patterned stone square. A traditional stone lamp on a pedestal stood on the grass, surrounded by a variety of low bushes thick with leaves. A weeping cherry tree grew by the fence, its branches drooping.

The houses evoked images of a quieter, calmer time before cars and planes and television and computers, and I understood why modern Japanese are fascinated by samurai style.

Though Isabella Bird did not explore the area, she was determined to travel on to Aomori and the sea. Setting out one morning when the rain stopped, she crossed several rivers whose waters were half-way up the horses' bodies. The mud-covered roads were so thickly covered with branches, logs, and puddles that she dismounted and walked ahead. To her surprise, she found a wide, new road that climbed up the mountain in easy zigzags. Reaching the top, she stopped to admire the view. Then it began to rain heavily again. Horrified, she saw that: "Trees of great size slid down, breaking others in their fall; rocks were rent and carried away trees in their descent, the waters rose before our eyes. Where the forest-covered hillside had been there was a great scar, out of which a torrent burst, which in half an hour carved for itself a deep ravine, and carried into the valley below an avalanche of stones and sand. The fine new road was torn away and, in one moment, a hundred yards of it disappeared."

Earthquakes and landslides still occur in this region of rivers, lakes, ravines, and mountains. Looking for the scenery she visited, I went to the Shiraiwadake Mountains to hike a trail into the dramatic Dakigaeri Gorge. The gorge is spectacular. Its soaring cliffs are almost perpendicular and rise on either side of a rushing river, which throws itself over the rocks and boulders along its path. The cliffs are peppered with shrubs and trees growing out at odd angles from the rocky surface.

But the untouched wilderness has been tamed. The gorge is a well-known tourist attraction. As I walked up the road toward it, I saw a parking lot filled with buses, trucks, vans and cars. A row of snack stores and souvenir places stands at the side, and just beyond, a paved path leads past picnic tables. To reach the trail that leads up to a waterfall, you cross a wooden suspension bridge. I was accompanied by dozens of other eager hikers exclaiming at the vivid green river that rushes far below the bridge.

The trail hugs a steep ravine's wall and winds past grass and shrubs. The surface was muddy and slick from the recent rains. It was barely wide enough for two people walking together. I set out, but I was not alone. On a Saturday morning, hundreds of other people were also eager to experience the beauty of the Dakigaeri Gorge. A young woman pushed a stroller with a crying baby, while her friend grabbed the hands of two small children who threatened to run to the edge and fall off. A woman in a fashionable calf-length, fitted black silk coat wore black high-heeled shoes as she walked up, accompanied by a man in a gray suit and tie and elegant leather shoes. An older woman stopped to wipe the mud off her white summer shoes with a white handkerchief. Three men in rain jackets climbed up slowly, using walking sticks. Half a dozen teenagers in jeans and tee-shirts with English phrases like "Florida Oranges" and "Hard Rock" skipped up the trail in their sneakers, talking, running, and laughing as they overtook people.

I walked for about an hour, looking at the views over the ravine, the green river and white foam far below, the jagged cliffs opposite, the rain-dripping trees along the way. There were people at every point along the trail, either in front of me so I overtook them, coming down so I paused to let them pass, or behind me talking. The noise of voices and the thump of feet on the ground almost drowned the roar of the river.

I sat down on a bench at the side. Upriver, spectacular churning water thrashed its way over a wide stretch of huge rocks, throwing white spray into the air. Downriver, the water gurgled as it rushed over boulders and rocks, pulling sticks and branches in its path. Lowering clouds hung in the sky, and a light drizzle fell. With my back to the trail, it was almost like being alone. On the opposite bank of the river, people had spread out blue tarpaulins and blankets and were enjoying picnics, despite the gray skies.

Though the rural country through which Isabella Bird rode was often deserted, when she reached a town, she was the center of attention. One evening, standing on the balcony of her room, huge crowds gathered to stare up at her. The house-master asked them to leave, but they replied: "It's neither fair nor neighborly of you to keep this great sight to yourself, seeing that our lives may pass without again looking on a foreign woman," and so they were allowed to stay. The next day, when she rode her horse through Yokote, an "ill-favored, ill-smelling, forlorn, dirty, damp, miserable place," the local residents rushed out from the communal bath house to see her, "men and women alike without a particle of clothing."

Today, the Tohuku residents keep their clothes on and are quite accustomed to foreigners. Few people gave me a second glance as I walked round the streets. One evening, I went into a tiny sushi bar for dinner. I sat at the solid wooden counter and looked around, feeling a little apprehensive. The only other people were a couple at the counter, both middle aged, who were talking and joking with the gray-haired chef and his wife. Outside the rain was pelting down on the narrow empty dark streets, yet inside it felt warm and friendly.

I ordered a sushi-sashimi serving, pickled plums, and a beer. The TV above the counter showed a baseball game, which the chef glanced up at every now and again. Pinned on the walls were photos of extremely fleshy sumo wrestlers and a calendar picture of a Japanese woman in a traditional kimono.

The man sitting at the end was very outgoing and friendly and asked who I was and what I was doing. It turned out that he and his wife were on vacation visiting her brother, the chef, and his wife, so they were all related. He asked me about my husband and my family, and I told them why I was traveling on my own and why I liked it. He offered to be my guide, but I said I didn't need another one. We all toasted each other's health several times. By the time I had eaten my sushi and finished my beer, the two women volunteered to join me on my travels and leave the husbands to look after the restaurant!

The next morning, I took the train from Kakunodate that followed much the same route Isabella Bird had taken. She crossed several rivers and found "a great plain, on which green billows of rice were rolling sunlit before a fresh north wind. The scenery, which is extremely pretty, gained everything from sunlight and color. It looked a simple, home-like region, a very pleasant land."

Today, farmlands stretch over the landscape. Steep slopes with tall evergreen fir trees crowd together. The harvested stalks of rice hang to dry on rails, on fences, and on sticks about six feet high, drooping like an overcoat from about half-way down. Some sticks had plastic hats on to protect the rice, like cone hats. Tall feathery fronds of grass edged the fields and waved in the wind as the train rushed by.

The sun came out from behind the clouds, and I glimpsed an old, thatched cottage farm house, a new farm house with a blue roof, persimmon trees thick with orange fruit, the back yards of houses close to the tracks with washing on the line. The train slowed down as we approached Hirosaki. It was still a simple, pleasant land.

Chapter 7 From Hirosaki to Aomori

Hirosaki is a castle town close to here, with a high-class college which has had two Americans for its headmasters. Three Christian students from there—remarkably intelligent-looking, handsomely-dressed young men, who all spoke a little English—said that they heard that an English lady was in the house, and asked if I were a Christian, but apparently were not satisfied, till, in answer to the question if I had a Bible, I was able to produce one.

Isabella Bird, Kuroishi, 1878

American World War II bombers left Hirosaki untouched, while reducing most of old Aomori to rubble, so Hirosaki is liberally splashed with bits of its feudal past — the temples, the castle gates (lightning got the castle itself), a few old houses and shops, and even the narrow winding roads. A mood of quiet refinement permeates the city in contrast to the harsh climate.

Exploring Tohuku, *Jan Brown, Weatherhill, 1982*

Hirosaki became a religious center when, in the 1600s, the Tsugaru lord of the region built an imposing temple, Chosho-ji, as a suitable burial place for his clan lords. After it was completed, he decreed that all the Zen temples in his domain should be brought to the same place, and a fortified temple town was created.

Over the centuries, other temples have been established there, and today several streets are lined with dozens of temples, new and old. I stayed in a modern temple on the second floor overlooking a crowded cemetery. The large, plain room had smooth tatami mats, cream colored wallpaper, two square neon ceiling lights with pull cords, two cups, tea, and a hot water thermos on a table, and an old television set. My bed was the rolled-up futon in the corner. Downstairs were basins, toilets, a shower, and a large old-fashioned bath.

Meals were served at a low table in the temple meeting room, which was startling in its lavish decorations. Everything was covered with glittering gold. Ornate gold chandeliers and large, turquoise-and-black domes hung from the ceiling. The raised altar on one side of the room had a towering Buddha in the center, sitting cross-legged and framed by a dark oval shell. Above him was a gold-covered tiered box bedecked with jangling bells and carved shapes. Gold ornaments and hangings filled the spaces on either side.

I went to visit the old temples, which stand along a wide avenue, and have carved doors and sculpted figures from mythology outside. Many of the temples are not open to the public. At the end of the road was a familiar *torii* gate that led into a complex of buildings, most of them closed, but a low building to the side had an open door.

I walked in to find myself facing an altar and an astonishing sight. Dozens of lifelike and almost life-size carved figures of men stood on either side of the central altar, like spectators at a baseball game. Arrayed in rows of three and four on descending stone steps, every face was individual, every expression unique, and each one wore something different. The statues and robes had remnants of vividly painted colors of deep red, clear blue, white, and gold visible under a thick layer of dust. Each figure had been carefully placed so it was visible from the front, like a group photograph. Some looked happy, some sad, some worried, some bored. One man was cheerily waving his left hand, while another held both hands out. Most robes were closely wrapped round the body, but one stood bare-chested at the front, his robe loosely hung around his waist. One held up a small, red Buddha figure. Most of the heads were bald, with long ears and ear-lobes, and the majority of the faces looked serious. Only one statue had shoulder-length hair and smiled sweetly, and one face was painted black.

These were the 500 disciples of Buddha. They looked so alive that I half-expected them to move. I sat on the wooden bench in front and looked from one to another, at the different expressions and personalities so clearly expressed in the carving. I felt very strange to be surrounded by so many lifelike people who had waited here for centuries and wondered how they were chosen to be included.

Isabella Bird never hid her passion for her Protestant faith, though she still visited Buddhist, Shinto, and other religious centers. One temple "differed little from a Roman Catholic church. The low altar, on which were lilies and lighted candles, was draped in blue and silver, and on the high altar, draped in crimson and cloth of gold, there was nothing but a closed shrine, an incense burner, and a vase of lotuses."

She was now resting from her travels and had found a comfortable room where she planned to stay for a few days. Only the sound of persistent drumming one evening enticed her outside to watch a local festival parade where "three monster drums nearly the height of a man's body, and strapped to the drummers, end upwards, and thirty small drums, all beaten rub-a-dub-dub without ceasing." Flatbeds on wheels decorated with huge figures were being pulled through the streets by hundreds of men, and she saw "a giant in brass armor killing a revolting-looking demon, a hunter, thrice the size of life, killing a wild horse equally magnified, and highly-colored gods and devils equally hideous."

Hirosaki today is still renowned for its lavish festivals. Its spectacular floats are kept on permanent display in a museum. The first float I saw hung from the ceiling of the visitor center. A giant, ferocious warrior in a gold helmet and armor, with large eyes, dark moustaches, and a war-like expression rode a galloping gray horse, which had wide, startled eyes, open mouth and pointed teeth, hoofs poised as if to jump to the floor below.

As I walked over to the float museum, I heard deep, rhythmic thumping, like a jackhammer on concrete, echo through the air. In a vast main hall were two huge drums, about eight feet high. A young man in a silk-embroidered jacket beat traditional rhythms with two long, thin, red wooden sticks: slow-slow-quick-quick-quick-slow, boom-boom-ba-ba-ba-boom, again and again. Invited to try, I copied the swinging gestures and forceful thumps as I hit the flat sides of the drums. Suddenly I could feel—as well as hear—the tremendous reverberations explode into the air like waves crashing in the sea. *Boom-boom-ba-ba-ba-boom!* The reverberations from the two drums filled the room, and floated out into the city streets. A second young man lifted a traditional Japanese flute to his lips and began to play a haunting melody, an eerie blending of the high notes of the flute and the booming drum beats.

The traditional floats are kept for display on high platforms, which tower almost to the ceiling. The bold, free-sculpted figures are dazzlingly painted in gold and red, blue and white, silver and scarlet. It's cartoon-style art with exaggerated shapes and mischievous details and a sense of unbridled exuberance, a celebration of devilish wickedness. Their artistry, color, vivacity, and drama are stunning.

There's a grotesque giant figure of Daikoku, the god of money and good fortune, his plump face ever-smiling above his round, shiny, bare belly. A devilish monster has the face of a leering monkey and raises its hairy arms threateningly. Opposite, a towering horse rears on a bridge, while his rider plunges a sword into a vicious dragon with pointed teeth and blood-red tongue. One float shows three wild figures with flowing, untidy red hair and long colorful robes around a huge cauldron, like the witches in Shakespeare's *Macbeth*. The exaggerated details—huge eyes, large bellies, violent expressions, vivid primary colors, teeth-baring monsters, long fingernails—are magnificent.

Though Isabella Bird chose not to go out, she sat at her window and watched as a woman in another house did her hair by adding swatches of false hair to create an elaborate hair style. A friend plucked the woman's eyebrows and removed the neck hairs with tweezers. Her face, ears, and neck were powdered white, and "with a camel's-hair brush she then applied some mixture to her eyelids to make the bright eyes look brighter, the teeth were blackened with a leather brush dipped in a solution of gall-nuts, and a patch of red was placed upon the lower lip."

Women today in Hirosaki no longer display white faces. The ones I saw wore modern make-up and clothes. I wandered into an exhibit of a local women's weaving club where I was invited to meet the members, who all looked attractive and well-dressed. The two women who showed me round had tastefully applied lipstick, eyeshadow, and blusher, and their faces were smoothly powdered. Their black hair was perfectly styled, one loose and curly, the other cut very short and close to the head. One wore a knee-length silk dress in pale gray with a leather belt. The other had on a soft, cream-colored suit with a silky yellow shirt and a scarf round her neck. Their earrings, bracelets, necklaces, high-heeled shoes and stockings were carefully chosen to complement their outfits.

The two women introduced me to the other members of the weaving group and their work displayed on long tables. There were woven baskets, bags, mats, hangings, animals, flowers, and even a basket with six woven baby birds. All the women were friendly, eager to know what I was doing and where I was going. They were intrigued to know how I was managing traveling on my own, and what my husband thought. The two women who showed me round both said they would love to visit America. As they took my card, they assured me they would come on their own because "we will leave our husbands behind, they are no fun, they work too hard, and they won't go on vacation!"

It was time to travel the final stretch to Aomori and over to the island of Hokkaido. Isabella Bird avoided horses and walking; instead, she bribed two men to pull her in a *kurama* carriage. Though the rain had stopped, the roads were muddy and difficult, and at one point she was thrown into a ditch. She emerged unhurt but soaked with water and mud. Finally, as she crossed the last ridge, she saw the ocean and exulted: "The gray sea was Aomori Bay—my long land-journey was done."

She and Ito managed to board the last ferry of the day. It should have taken a few hours to reach the island but, as the boat left the harbor and entered the Tsugaru Strait, a gale struck with tremendous force. The journey to Hokkaido took fourteen hours to cover sixty miles. She had expected to be met, but the British Consulate officials assumed the ferry would not run in the storm, so no one came to the dock. The indefatigable Isabella Bird marched to a Church Mission House where an English couple whom she had met in Tokyo had invited her to stay with them.

"I was unfit to enter a civilized dwelling," she wrote. "My clothes, besides being soaked, were coated and splashed with mud up to the top of my hat. My gloves and boots were finished, my mud-splashed baggage was soaked with salt water. But I felt a somewhat legitimate triumph at having conquered all obstacles, and having accomplished more than I intended to accomplish when I left."

Today, there are several ways to reach the island of Hokkaido. Planes fly to Sapporo Airport, ferries and hydrofoils cross the water, and there's a train under the Tsugaru Strait through the Seikan Submarine Tunnel, which opened in 1988.

I chose the new train tunnel, which takes about two-and-a-half hours. As the train approached the tunnel, announcements in Japanese and English provided information. It's 33.5 miles long, the longest railway tunnel ever built under the ocean, with 14.5 miles under the sea. It's also the deepest, 787 feet below sea level at the deepest point. There are two stations inside the tunnel, and some trains stop to allow passengers to take a two-hour museum tour.

We rushed through several short tunnels, then a longer tunnel, and then another short tunnel, and came out again into the daylight. A young boy sitting opposite with his mother kept asking if this was THE tunnel, and she kept shaking her head. In the drizzling rain, we crossed wide rivers, passed more farms, saw mountains draped in mist. The clouds looked lower and darker than before.

After more announcements, the train plunged into the darkness, and stayed there. The Seikan Tunnel took about twenty-five minutes to zip through, but it didn't seem particularly exciting. It felt like the London Underground or the New York City subway. The other passengers were unperturbed and read their newspapers and books, napped, ate snacks, or chatted to each other as we traveled under the ocean. The young boy peered steadfastly out of the window, as if hoping to see some fish. There were only speeding black walls and the rumbling noise of the train.

We came out into daylight, and announcements welcomed us to the island of Hokkaido. The train rushed through more short tunnels. We sped past farms and villages where rice was stacked to dry in cone-shaped shocks, or hung from bars like spaghetti drying, and on poles like small trees. Bright blue waterproof tarpaulins covered farm equipment, flapped on barn roofs, or protected crops on the ground.

As I looked out, I glimpsed a slice of gray-blue water stretching to the horizon. It was the ocean between Hokkaido and the mainland. Every now and then I caught sight of the sea as the train rushed on past fields of rice, irrigation channels, dark evergreens close together, and bales of hay wrapped in black plastic. Approaching Hakodate station, the fields were replaced by the buildings, houses, and streets of the town. The train slowed down and finally stopped at the platform. I had arrived on time, relaxed, and—unlike Isabella—perfectly dry. I was ready to explore Hokkaido and find the Ainu with my new guide.

Isabella
Bird
Memorials
in
Yamagata

Nikko

In 1878, Isabella Bird visited the temples of Nikko and wrote about the Pagoda, above, the Wind God, opposite, and the frieze of the Three Wise Monkeys, still there to see today.

The flute player and the fearsome demons contrast with the simple style of the samurai room. Below are carved figures of Buddhist disciples.

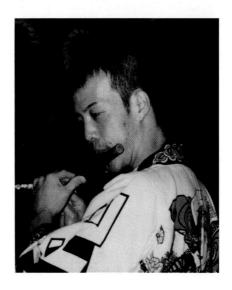

Hirosaki

Japanese women are as diverse as women anywhere. Above, two farm women in Kitakata. Above right, a tourist official who was getting married the next day. Below, actors from the Waribi-za Theatre.

Women in Japan

Above, at the Ha-
kodate fish market,
the stall owner was
sure that I could
take a crab with me
on my travels!
On the right, the
two women in tra-
ditional kimonos
were visiting the
Yokohama Silk
Museum.

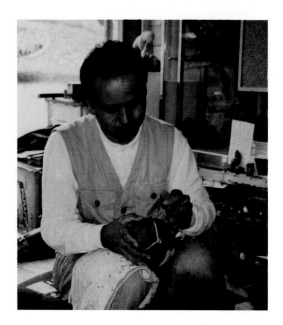

Ainu

Above, a woodworker in Biratori.
Below, dancers in Shiraoi village.

Chapter 8
Hakodate

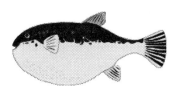

I find the climate here on Hokkaido more invigorating than on the main island. It is Japan, but yet there is a difference somehow. When the mists lift they reveal not mountains smothered in greenery, but naked peaks, volcanoes only recently burned out. Hakodate itself makes one feel that it is Japan all over. The streets are very wide and clean, but the houses are mean and low.

Isabella Bird, 1878

The gateway to South Hokkaido is Hakodate, a city that quietly breathes of history and romanticism. An exotic mood floats on the breeze. The magnificence of nature can be enjoyed fully throughout the seasons. The roads are endlessly straight, and there is unlimited variation in the view of the sea and mountains. The way to travel is to leisurely walk around and explore the city.

Tourist brochure, 1998

When Isabella Bird arrived at the British Consulate after her night at the Church Mission, officials fell over themselves to welcome the famous Miss Bird. She settled comfortably into her room overlooking the harbor and began to prepare for her inland journey. To her surprise, a British botanist told her he had hired Ito as his assistant for $7 a month, but Ito ran away when she offered $12 a month! Isabella Bird assured him that when she completed her trip, Ito could join him and noted, "Ito's Shinto creed has not taught him any better."

For my week exploring Hokkaido, I hired an American guide, Annette, who had lived in Japan for seven years studying pottery. She spoke Japanese and was eager to help me track Isabella Bird's footsteps and find the Ainu. Even though she now lived in Colorado with her husband, we met for the first time at Sapporo airport on Hokkaido when she arrived from Tokyo.

I liked her immediately. A round faced woman with dark curly hair, Annette had an easy smile and a relaxed approach to life. Living in Japan had given her a slightly jaded view of the country and its problems, which was a good antidote to my uncritical enthusiasm.

We took a train to Hakodate and stayed at a Japanese pension near the waterfront. The rooms were bright and clean with twin beds. Hot showers, flush toilets, and coin washing machines were down the hall. In a sunny downstairs room, the breakfast buffet every morning offered platters and bowls of green salad, pickled green beans, grapes, sliced bananas, sliced cheese and ham, scrambled eggs, plain yogurt, croissants, and containers of butter and marmalade, as well as orange juice, tea, coffee, and iced water. The room had a dozen tables. The other guests included a Japanese couple with a little boy who pushed bananas into his mouth happily, a Chinese woman with a young girl who sat on her lap, a thin-faced man sitting alone, a young couple gazing at each other adoringly, and two elderly couples who squeezed into a booth against the wall and talked loudly. We were the only non-Asians, and our table by the window overlooked a garden courtyard.

Hakodate, Yokohama, and Nagasaki were the first three port cities opened when Japan's isolation ended in 1859. Hakodate, Isabella Bird noted when she arrived almost twenty years later, stretched for two miles along the shore, "and has climbed the hill till it can go no higher. The houses are nothing but tinder. Nearly every house is a shop, and most supply only the ordinary articles. Real or imitated foreign goods abound, and the only novelties are the furs, skins, and horns. I covet the great bear furs, and the deep cream-colored furs of the Ainu dogs, which are cheap as well as handsome."

Today, Hakodate is a busy international port, with a population of more than 300,000. Like San Francisco, the houses climb up steep roads from the bay where boats fill the harbor, converted warehouses on the waterfront are filled with stores and restaurants, and street cars clatter along the main roads. The shops sell products from China, Korea, Europe, and South America, as well as from Japan, and there are dozens of different places to eat.

The first place to visit was the daily fish market. Set on the waterfront, the market now attracts more than 400 vendors who arrive at 4 a.m. In the bright mid-morning sunshine, colorful awnings and umbrellas shaded glass tanks filled with sharp-clawed crabs, boxes filled with squid, octopus, and eels spread one on top of the other, a gleaming quilt of gray, beige, white, brown, yellow, purple, and green—eyes open, mouths whiskered, fins drooping.

As I walked past a fish tank stuffed to the brim with crabs and lobsters, their legs waving and eyes popping, a young man took out a couple, one small and the other large. Annette talked to him and then translated for me indignantly: "The small ones came from Japan and the big ones from Russia, because the Japanese over-fished the waters around Japan so there are no fish left, and they have to go to Russian waters."

The young man smiled at her comment, but didn't contradict it. I walked past other stalls that displayed dried fish in shades of pale red and deep brown stacked in rows or packed in boxes. There were containers of expensive red caviar eggs, fish placed in white boxes, small fish neatly lined up on top of larger fish on top of giant fish, fish packed in plastic, dried fish in foil packets, clams wrapped in heart-shaped clam shells, souvenir postcards, and gifts. One stall sold squid ice-cream! The sights, sounds, and smells of fish and sea were exhilarating after being inland for so long. They reminded me of buying a lobster on a fishing pier in Maine and eating it fresh cooked at a picnic table while waves crashed on the rocks below.

Farther along the quay stood colorful stalls laden with buckets and vases of fresh flowers in pink and white, mauve and orange, yellow and periwinkle. Golden fat melons spread in rows next to mounds of green beans, onions, squash, eggplant, garlic, and other vegetables. It smelled fresh and pungent. Mountains of cleaned potatoes, a specialty of the area at this time of year, filled several stalls, their creamy skins glowing.

The men and women vendors were friendly, talkative people. They bantered with the Japanese locals buying fish, watching as they picked, weighed, and compared them. Three women put a gray lobster on the scales and discussed its size and suitability as it threatened to climb off. A friendly woman in a red and black striped sweater and a denim apron assertively handed me slices of her specialty melons in two varieties. They were both sweet, juicy, delicious. She gave me a cooked piece of gray crab, which was the freshest, sweetest meat I've ever had, fleshy, soft, and perfect. Reluctantly, I said I couldn't take a melon or a crab with me, but I took her photo and promised to send it to her.

It's a pleasant stroll along the road by the waterfront with its old warehouses and low buildings. The red brick facade of the old Meijikan Post Office has been completely restored. Inside is an attractive mini-mall with a glassware studio, a music box shop, pizza snack bar, and souvenir shops. The outsides of other tall brick warehouses still stand, but they too have been transformed inside: boutiques sell pottery, woodwork, clothes, jewelry, art and souvenirs, and there are cafés, snack bars, and restaurants. As I strolled round one evening, loud American rap music poured out of loudspeakers that hung from the ceiling. When I went into a Japanese beer hall for the fish dinner special, the same music flooded the room, where stolid-faced men drank beer at a circular bar in the center.

Isabella Bird loved Hakodate and "though my tour is all planned and my arrangements are made, I linger on from day to day," she wrote. On a day trip on horseback, she admired "a glorious view of Hakodate Head looking like an island in the deep blue sea."

Today, Mount Hakodate is still spectacular. At dusk, the locals go to the top and watch the sun set. The winding mountain road to the summit is jammed with traffic. The steep cable car is much quicker. Sightseers by the dozens stand at the railings looking out over the bay far below: chattering groups of schoolgirls in uniforms, tourists with video-cameras, young boys peering into the telescopes, businessmen in suits and ties, families with strollers, and older people talking. On the evening I went, the sky was covered with hazy clouds, and the setting sun turned the misty horizon a deep pinky orange. The vivid color was reflected in the gray waters of the bay. As the lights of the city appeared, twinkling in the pale mist, people cheered and clapped, and there was a vigorous whirring and clicking of cameras.

The British Consulate still stands on a steep hill overlooking the harbor. It burned down twice after Isabella Bird's visit; the present building dates from 1913, and it was officially closed in 1934. In 1992, the building was re-opened as a historic attraction.

In front stands a statue of Mr. Eusden, the British Consul whom Isabella Bird met, and whom she praised because "he worked upon the powers that be with such good effect that the Governor has granted me a *shomon*, a sort of official letter or certificate, giving me a right to obtain horses and coolies everywhere at the Government rate, with a prior claim to accommodation at the houses kept up for officials on their circuits, and to help and assistance from officials generally."

Inside on the first floor is an English Tea Room and a gift shop selling British products such as lemon curd, Paddington Bear toys, china teacups, and books about the royal family. In the old main hall is a replica of the *Pawhatan*, one of American Commodore Matthew C. Perry's fleet of ships, and an entertaining diorama in a glass case about the arrival of the first Americans. Other exhibits upstairs describe the lives of those in the first British community, including Sir Thomas Blakiston, a trader who built the first lumber mill, and John Milne, a seismology professor from England who married a Buddhist priest's daughter in 1881.

I went up the narrow staircase to the third floor and was thrilled to find several rooms had been restored to look as they did in the 19th century when the Consulate was in service. The Consul's office had an imposing desk and chair, a rug on the floor, and a long telescope looking out at the boats in the harbor. At the end of the corridor were guest bedrooms. I peeked into one, which had a four-poster bed, a chair, a bureau, a mirror, and long windows that opened onto a balcony. It was easy to imagine Isabella Bird living here, writing her letters, studying her maps, and planning her trip. Along the corridor was the spacious living room. I walked in and looked up at the official photograph of a plump and elderly Queen Victoria that hung over the fireplace. In the center of the room stood a long, narrow, dark wooden table with plain upright wooden chairs around it.

On her last evening in Hakodate, Isabella Bird was invited to attend a dinner party in the British Consulate, and this was probably the room where it was held. The other guests whom she met were Count Diesbach of the French Legation, Mr. Von Siebold of the Austrian Legation, and Lieutenant Kreitner of the Austrian Army. The three men boasted of their plans to explore the interior of Hokkaido, measure the heights of the mountains, and find the sources of the rivers. She sat quietly with the Consul, Mr. Eusden, and his wife at the table as the men bragged about their extensive provisions, the wine they were taking, and their equipment.

She knew only too well what to expect in Japan after her months of travel. She smiled to herself and wrote later: "They are well prepared in food and claret, but take such a number of pack-ponies with them that I predict that they will fail, and that I, who have reduced my luggage to 45 pounds, will succeed! I hope to start on my long-projected tour tomorrow. I have planned it for myself with the confidence of an expert traveler, and look forward to it with great pleasure."

I too was ready to leave Hakodate and follow her trail as she looked for the Ainu tribes.

Chapter 9
Finding the Ainu

I am once again in the wilds! I am sitting outside an upper room built out almost over a lonely lake, with wooded points purpling and still shadows deepening in the sinking sun. I am not yet off the beaten track, but my spirits are rising with the fine weather, the drier atmosphere, and the freedom.
Isabella Bird on Hokkaido, 1878

Hokkaido offers wide-open landscapes for hikers, skiers, and bicyclists, as well as glimpses of vanishvanishing Ainu culture and relics of Hokkaido's frontier days. Japanese national parks often contain highly developed towns and populated areas, so it takes some effort to find the unspoiled spots within them."
Gateway to Japan, 1998

When Isabella Bird set off to see Hokkaido, or Yezo, as it was then called, the island was still virtually unexplored. The Japanese Government's new policy of encouraging settlements had resulted in a few farms being established along the coast. Isabella Bird's plan was to travel into the interior, which she heard was "covered with forest matted together by lianas, and with an undergrowth of scrub bamboo impenetrable except to the axe, varied by swamps equally impassable, which give rise to hundreds of rivers well stocked with fish."

From Hakodate, she rode her horse along "a most displeasing road most of the way, with deep corrugations, and in the middle a high causeway of earth." After a pleasant night in a room by a lake, she set off along a sandy track, "through monotonous forest and swamp, with the volcano on one side and low wooded hills on the other. There are no villages, but several very poor tea-houses, and on the other side of the road, long sheds with troughs hollowed out like canoes containing horse food."

Her goal was to find the primitive tribes of Ainu who, she hoped, would provide her with excellent material to write about to prove she was an explorer not merely a travel writer. She had been told the Ainu were "complete savages in everything but their disposition, which is said to be so gentle and harmless that I may go among them with perfect safety."

The word Ainu means "human." The original inhabitants of Japan, the Ainu do not look at all Japanese. They have round eyes, round swarthy faces, a quantity of thick dark hair, and are about the same height as the Japanese. Their language, religion, and culture are unique. It's thought that the first Ainu traders were hunters and fishermen descended from the Jomon culture that dominated Japan about 2,000 years ago. Then they became the trade intermediaries between the Korean, Russian, Chinese, Manchurian, and Dutch traders. But during the eighteenth and nineteenth centuries, as the Japanese merchants became more powerful, the Ainu declined. In 1868, the new Meiji government prohibited the Ainu from hunting and fishing, banned their language, and forbade their customs such as bear worship and tattooing.

As she traveled into Muroran, Isabella Bird was thrilled to see her first Ainu houses and people in a village where Ainu and Japanese lived together. She was surprised that the Ainu houses were made of reeds tied to a wooden frame, with small windows and thatched roofs, rather like Polynesian huts, and thought them unsuitable for the harsh winters of the north. She noticed a group of young Ainu men, who "were young and beardless, their lips were thick, and their mouths very wide, and I thought that they approached more nearly to the Eskimo type than to any other. They had masses of soft black hair falling on each side of their faces."

Suddenly, she saw Count Diesbach, one of the men with whom she had dined at the British Consulate and who had been so confident as he set out, riding toward her. He leapt from his horse, shouting about the fleas, the discomforts, the agonies of travel. With him was Benri, the chief of the Biratori Ainu village. After she had been introduced, Benri said she could stay at the village until he returned in a few days. She set off immediately with Ito and an Ainu guide.

Biratori was the largest of the Ainu settlements, set amid forests and mountains, along the Saru river. She thought that "a lonelier place could scarcely be found." She was taken to the chief's house, where his nephew sat her at the place of honor by the fire and arranged for her luggage and bed to be placed behind a reed screen at the side.

Her stay in the chief's house lasted three days. It was the highlight of her journey and later formed the major part of her book. She wrote down every detail of the daily life she observed with such accuracy that her descriptions are as vivid as when she first saw them. She saw the clothes the Ainu made from woven elm tree bark, their carved wooden utensils, as well as their shoes and jewelry. She learned how every year a woman raised a bear cub that was later killed in a ritual ceremony as part of Ainu bear worship. The Ainu worshipped all animals and believed them to be gods. In the evening, the older men, with long beards, sat round the fire and, after sake was poured into their bowls, laid a sacred stick across the bowl, and slowly drank after much waving and dipping of sticks to the god.

On the third day, the men took her to see their sacred shrine on a nearby cliff. As they stood silently before the altar in the simple building, Chief Benri suddenly appeared. He had not wanted the villagers to talk to her before he returned and exploded in fury. Later, she spent time with him, confirming what she had been told. She thought him intelligent, but she saw he had complete control over the lives of the villagers. "His manner to all the men is like that of a master to slaves, and they bow when they speak to him. No one can marry without his approval. If anyone builds a house he chooses the site. He compels restitution of stolen property, and in all cases he fixes the fines which are to be paid by the delinquents." She added wryly: "He has some fine qualities, but he is a brute and a sot."

An American researcher, Romyn Hitchcock, visited Biratori some years later while researching the Ainu on behalf of the Smithsonian Institution in Washington, D.C. He met the old Chief Benri and watched the traditional sake ceremony. Benri, he noticed, "took the largest share of the sake, for he not only had a large cup, but it was filled quite to the brim." Hitchcock asked him about Isabella Bird, and Benri described her as "the woman to whom he told so many lies."

Isabella Bird had revised her idealized view of the simple life of a native: "The glamor which at first disguises the inherent barrenness of savage life has had time to pass away, and I see it in all its nakedness as a life not much raised about the necessities of animal existence, timid, monotonous, barren of good, dark, dull, without hope, and without God in the world." She saw the Ainu as "knowing nothing, hoping nothing, fearing a little, the need for clothes and food the one motive principle, sake in abundance the one good!" but admitted that they were "truthful, and, on the whole, chaste, hospitable, honest, reverent, and kind to the aged." She concluded: "They are charming in many ways, but make one sad, too, by their stupidity, apathy, and hopelessness, and all the sadder that their numbers appear to be increasing; and as their physique is very fine, there does not appear to be a prospect of the race dying out at present."

Today the train from Hakodate follows the curve of the bay passing villages and farms, stopping at stations with a single platform and a few people waiting. From the train window I caught sudden glimpses of the blue ocean, birds sitting on the waves, a fishing boat bobbing in the distance. The sandy beaches looked neglected, littered with driftwood. Along the road by the sea were dingy industrial buildings and small stores. I left the train and drove round the bay to reach Biratori.

The peninsula is a beautiful rural area of rolling hills and valleys known as the Kentucky of Japan because it's the home of the horse industry. Unlike the Japanese packhorses Isabella Bird encountered, thoroughbred horses are raised here. Magnificent black and bay and gray horses, with long legs, elegant heads, and beautifully trimmed manes, graze peacefully in the lush, green fields. Japanese tourists often visit the barns and can even stay at a Wild West Ranch in the region where Japanese wranglers teach them cowboy skills.

Biratori lies inland. The main highway leads past low buildings, small stores, and houses on side streets with trees, gardens and hedges. The town has some 500 residents. About 85 percent of them are of Ainu descent. There are now about 25,000 Ainu descendants on Hokkaido, and an estimated 200,000 throughout Japan.

The Ainu survived through many years of persecution. Shigeru Kayano, an Ainu who grew up here in the 1930s, has been a major figure in preserving Ainu traditions, which are now enjoying a rebirth. He was elected to Biratori Town Assembly, where he served for 17 years, and later was appointed to the Japanese Diet (or Parliament) in 1994, the first Ainu to serve there. He was the fifth candidate in a political contest for four seats. When one candidate dropped out, he was appointed to that seat. He has compiled an Ainu dictionary, written his autobiography called *Our Land was a Forest,* as well as other books, and established Ainu language classes.

When he was a young man, he saw that assimilation was destroying the traditions and culture of his people. He quietly began collecting the arts, crafts, costumes, tools, and other materials before they disappeared. As his collection grew, he realized he needed somewhere to keep it and raised money for a museum. It opened in June 1972. Today, the Kayano Shigeru Ainu Memorial Museum is set at the end of narrow road off the main Biratori highway.

Weather-beaten, thatched Ainu huts and a storehouse on stilts stand outside. Each hut has a fireplace in a pit, a raised platform beside it, a hanging shelf of wood and straw, and patterned mats on the floor. The museum building displays Ainu robes, a hollowed log boat, arrows, prayer sticks, fish hooks, spear points, cups, bowls, earrings, and much more in several crowded rooms. In addition, there are materials from American Indians, Australian aborigines, Caribbean Indians, and other indigenous people. During the United Nations Decade of the Indigenous People, an Ainu conference was held here.

The Nibutani Ainu Culture Museum is a couple of miles away. The new museum was built in 1991 with funds given to the Ainu after a controversy about a dam that flooded traditional lands. In 1997, a lawsuit over the dam was settled, with a landmark ruling that the dam had violated Saru Lake Ainu rights, and which recognized the Ainu as the indigenous people of Japan.

The Nibutani Museum sits beside the new lake. It is a striking modern building with a high peaked roof that soars above the exhibit space inside. Well-lit display areas spread out like a fan from an oval central hall with curving sitting areas. On gleaming wooden platforms stand wooden and glass shelves and cases displaying knives and tools for carving and weaving, shoes made of salmon skins, a bucket made of woven bark, long wood posts with frills of curled wood shavings at the tops which were household gods, necklaces, brooches, a log boat, fishing gear, and ceremonial items. Traditional Ainu robes hang on a rail in a pull-out drawer so you can feel as well as see the embroidery and texture. Two TV monitors show videos—music sung round an Ainu camp fire, a song about water, a traditional story told by an old man—in a comfortable viewing corner. I was astonished that in both museums the Ainu artifacts and traditions which Isabella Bird had described so accurately looked so familiar that I could recognize them immediately.

After I had toured the museum, the director, a slim young man with thick, dark hair, came out to meet me. I told him what I was doing, and he knew all about Isabella Bird. He showed me his copy of her book and copied pages about her from an encyclopedia. We discussed the importance of her impact on the Ainu and how she is still remembered by them. He felt that another British researcher who was in Japan soon after Isabella Bird, Dr. Neil Gordon Munro, was even more important.

Munro, who worked as a doctor in a Tokyo hospital, spent his later years in Biratori living with the Ainu and wrote a definitive work about their lives which is still in print.

As I left, I noticed two distinctive life-size wooden figures of an Ainu man and woman outside a souvenir store on the main road. Inside were aisles with ashtrays, bowls, keyrings, postcards, plastic toys, dolls, pens and pencils, carved horses, and boxes filled with hand-carved wooden owls, deer, and bears, painted or in natural wood.

At the side of the doorway was a raised platform. A young man sat cross-legged carving a solid lump of wood. His dark eyes were round, and his eyebrows thick and dark. His black hair was combed back and thinning at the front. His skin was smooth and dark. Though he was clean shaven, there was a shadow on his chin and cheeks where a beard might easily grow. He wore blue jeans, sneakers, and a white long-sleeved tee-shirt, over which, like an apron, was a cotton vest with pockets. He never looked up as I stood watching. I politely asked if I could talk to him and he nodded.

"Yes, I am Ainu, and I am a traditional woodcarver," he told me. "I carve owls and other animals. I work here every day. I learned to carve from my father, and he learned from his father. Today I use much the same tools, not that different from the old ones." He waved a hand to the tools hanging behind him and then added: "All that I make is for sale here."

Just in front of him, at a table, three women sat shelling a bowl of nuts. A little boy ran around playing with a toy airplane.

"That is my mother, my wife, and a cousin," he said, "and the boy is my son." The women smiled and nodded. The family lives in a house in town, as they have for many years. The children go to local schools. Today, they are part of the modern world of tourism, creating crafts and selling them to visitors to make a living. As we talked, he avoided looking up, keeping his eyes modestly down. Though he allowed me to take a photograph, he would not look at the camera but kept carving.

I looked along the shelves and chose a wooden owl with pale round eyes and a dark brown head. The owl is an important god because it is the protector of the village, the only animal with a specific duty. I showed the owl to the woodcarver. He nodded, and said yes, he had made it. With great care, he carved his name, the place, and the date in Japanese years on the bottom, and gave it to me with a smile.

I paid his wife, and we all smiled and bowed. He picked up his block of wood from the floor among the curling white shavings, chose a tool, and scraped at the wood, as his family had done for generations.

Chapter 10
Shiraoi
Ainu

Shiraoi consists of a large old lodge, and about eleven Japanese houses, most are which are sake shops, a fact which supplies an explanation of the squalor of the Ainu village of fifty-two houses on the shore.

Isabella Bird, 1878

Shiraoi, the town, was established in 1856. The city was originally a center for Ainu culture, the original inhabitants who were conquered by the Japanese about 150 years ago. The town slogan:"The city of positive thinking, advancement of culture, and promotion of an active lifestyle," summarizes its philosophy.

Shiraoi-Quesnel Sister City Website, 1998

By the time Isabella Bird left Biratori on horseback to ride along the bay to Shiraoi, she had completely changed her views about Ainu life. On the day she left she saw drunken Ainu rolling about, and "tipsy men were staggering about and falling flat on their backs, to lie there like dogs till they were sober." Indignant, she made a speech to the Biratori villagers telling them to give up alcohol. They replied: "We must drink to the gods, or we shall die," to which Chief Benri nodded agreement.

She was appalled at their attitude and exclaimed: "Beastly intoxication is the highest happiness to which these poor savages aspire," and then added philosophically: "It was a sad scene, yet one to be matched in a hundred places in Scotland every Saturday afternoon."

Brought up as a devout Christian and a minister's daughter, Isabella Bird did not understand why the Ainu offered prayers to the god of fire, the god of windows, and many others. In her most severe condemnation of the Ainu, she concluded: "It is nonsense to write of the religious ideas of a people who have none, and of beliefs among people who are merely adult children. I have taken infinite trouble to learn from them what their religious notions are, and the whole sum is a few vague fears and hopes, and a suspicion that there are things outside themselves more powerful than themselves, whose good or evil influences may be influenced by libations of sake."

Doubtful that missionaries could help the Ainu, she thought that "a medically-trained nurse, who would give medicines and proper food, with proper nursing, would save many lives and much suffering.

It is of no use to tell these people to do anything which requires to be done more than once; they are just like children."

Despite her criticisms, the freedom of the Ainu women impressed her. Though the women did all the hard work including drawing water, chopping wood, grinding millet, and cultivating the soil, yet, she noted: "They look cheerful, and even merry when they smile, and are not like the Japanese, prematurely old. They eat of the same food, and at the same time as the men, laugh and talk before them, and received equal support and respect in old age. They sell mats and bark-cloth, and the husbands do not take their earnings from them."

She learned that the black tattoos on their upper lips and arms began at the age of five, when ash was rubbed into a cut on the upper lip, and then added to every year until they married.

In Biratori, marriage was permitted between women over seventeen, and men over twenty-one. The couple first asked the chief for approval, and then the man asked the girl's father if he could marry her. The betrothal was celebrated with drinking sake and exchanging gifts. Afterwards the man found a house for the couple away from their parents.

Once, riding in her *kurama* carriage, Isabella Bird overtook four young Ainu women walking barefoot and watched as "after a good deal of laughing with the men, they took hold of my *kurama* and the whole seven raced with it at full speed for half a mile, shrieking with laughter."

When I was spoke with an American man married to an Ainu woman about the differences between Ainu and Japanese women, he said that Ainu women always had more freedom, adding: "Women and men are used to independence, particularly in marriage, because Ainu women were never taught to be subservient like Japanese women."

Isabella Bird rode on to Shiraoi, the next Ainu village, set on the shores of a lake. The houses resembled the grass huts in Hawaii and "in their houses, as in their faces, the Ainu are more European than their conquerors, as they possess doorways, windows, central fireplaces, and raised sleeping places." Each house had its entrance set in the west, the storage area in the east, and three windows, with a sacred window facing the entrance for the gods.

She was shocked at the poverty of the village, where there were no fields to cultivate, "but fish-oil and fish-manure are made in immense quantities, and, though it is not the season here, the place is pervaded by an ancient and fish-like smell. The houses are much smaller, poorer, and dirtier than those of Biratori."

Going into several of the houses, she found they "looked like dens, and, as it was raining, husband, wife, and five or six naked children, all as dirty as could be, with unkempt locks, were huddled round the fires." In the storehouses, fish and venison hung from the rafters, "and the smell of these and the stinging of the smoke were most trying."

When I reached Shiraoi, it was a modern city with a population of 20,000. It has cattle ranches, a fishing industry, businesses growing shiitake mushrooms, and a large paper mill. But at first sight, as the bus wound along the flat coast road into Shiraoi, the view was depressing. Jutting out onto the beaches were small factories and gravel pits. Along the roads were rundown houses, and an imposing industrial complex puffed thick fumes into the air.

Annette sniffed and said: "The Japanese ruin their beaches just like they ruin everything that's natural," and she expounded on their inability to appreciate nature and preserve the natural environment just as it is. The bus entered town along roads lined with low office buildings, garages, and dozens of small shops and stores. We got off near the Ainu village, which was across the road at the end of a quiet side street.

As the Shiraoi Ainu assimilated into Japanese society, their original lakefront village was abandoned. In 1976, the Shiraoi Foundation for the Preservation of Ainu Culture was established to create "educational promotion projects to transmit, preserve, research and study Ainu culture." In 1984, they opened a Folk Museum, with some five thousand Ainu folk materials as well as articles from Eskimo and other northern groups. The museum library has about one hundred Ainu paintings and some six thousand publications.

In 1990, after several years of work, an Ainu village, completely restored to look the way it did in the past, was opened as an educational and visitor center. Set on the shores of Lake Poroto, it's called Poroto Kotan. Kotan is the Ainu word for village.

On the sunny fall day I visited, I strolled past tall reeds that edge a wide lake, where dugout canoes floated, to the museum entrance. Placed in a wide semi-circle along the shore were beautiful thatched reed houses, looking as if they had just been built.

The village area was landscaped with tall trees, shrubs, colorful flower beds, and grassy lawns, with pathways between the houses. Picnic tables sat under the trees. A giant, black statue of a village elder, wearing traditional Ainu robes, loomed above.

Descendants of the Ainu give educational presentations, reenact ceremonies and provide information for visitors. As I walked around, I had a tangible sense of the friendship, closeness, security, and community that would have existed in the village; it reminded me of living in a tiny mountain town in Colorado. Here, every individual was part of the group, had a strong sense of belonging, knew his or her place, and worked for survival.

I walked into one of the huts. It was spacious and open, larger than other huts I had seen, like the main hut where Isabella Bird stayed, with smooth matting underfoot, and rows of benches waiting for visitors. On a platform was the traditional open fireplace with a black pot on top, where they used to cook stews for dinner. The only modern additions were framed photographs of people and scenes from the Ainu past.

Ainu music and dance did not impress Isabella Bird. She thought the wooden mouth harp "discordant," their songs only chants, and the dances were "slow and mournful." Their songs were chanted because the Ainu had no alphabet or written language, so their legends, tales, and stories were handed down orally from generation to generation, and chanted by the fireside while the narrator beat rhythmically with a stick. The women had their own oral tradition, which was handed down through groups of women, and they beat rhythms and chanted songs in chorus.

In the center of Poroto Kotan, on a raised circular stage surrounded by colorful flowers, daily performances of songs and dances are presented. I watched fascinated as a woman in a traditional robe decorated with geometric patterns and wearing a matching wide headband, played the wooden mouth harp, with its wailing, haunting notes, to begin the dance performance. Accompanied by harp, drums, and singing, a dozen men and women in embroidered robes, sandals, and head-dresses performed a variety of traditional dances. There was a circle dance, an intricate ceremonial dance to send a bear's spirit back to the gods, and a sword-swinging dance for men with much shouting, clashing blades, and brandishing weapons, to intimidate the evil gods. The dancers swirled round the raised, open-air stage, their costumes swinging as they turned, clapping hands and stamping their feet enthusiastically. The words of the old songs Isabella Bird heard a century ago echoed in the air as they re-created the music, movements, and steps. It was an exhilarating performance, and I joined with the audience sitting round the stage and clapped enthusiastically.

Afterwards, I spoke to the dancers. One of them, a young man of twenty-three, explained: "I am half Ainu. My mother is Ainu and my father is Japanese. I have always lived in Shiraoi. When I heard about the dance classes, I came along to learn. Now I perform as a dancer. It is my full-time job, and I have been doing it for a year."

He introduced his teacher, the choreographer, a slim dark-haired woman. She wore a cotton checked shirt and blue cotton pants, and no make-up. She is also part Ainu and began learning the dances 13 years ago with another group, and explained: "I was invited to be the teacher for this group. We have learned a great many dances, and there are actually twelve different styles. For festivals and ceremonies, we perform special dances. For the show, we do a selection of dances which we present six times a day."

The dancers make their own costumes, copying traditional patterns and designs. In the nineteenth century, the Ainu bought cotton fabric from the Japanese to make their robes and added appliqué and embroidery designs in the geometric patterns that are traditional. Isabella Bird admired Ainu clothes, particularly elm tree bark coats which looked "a durable and beautiful fabric in various shades of natural buff, and resembles canvas." Under the coats, men and women wore skin or bark-cloth vests, and fitted leggings, either of bark cloth or skin. The men's coats reached to just below the knees, tied with a belt with their knives attached, while the women's coats reached to the ankles and were fastened at the throat.

I asked the choreographer if she had heard of Isabella Bird. She nodded: "I have read her book in Japanese. It's in the museum bookstore."

The young man said thoughtfully: "Isabella Bird? You, know, I remember my grandparents talking about her."

In the museum were old photographs, paintings, and drawings, displays of bowls, kimonos, prayer sticks, and other artifacts of Ainu daily life. The most intriguing exhibit was a 1925 movie of an Ainu village showing black-and-white footage of women setting up looms and weaving bark cloth, cooking over open fires, children playing together, and men catching fish with a net. It was an astonishing view of people still following primitive ways at a time when films, photography, telephones, airplanes, cars, radio and electricity were transforming the world outside.

I went to see the museum director. Though he had been showing a group round, he took time to have a cup of coffee at a low table in his office. We talked about Isabella Bird. He had a copy of her book in Japanese and knew it well. He apologized for not being able to show me round but that day, a film crew had arrived and needed his help. I asked him who they were.

"They are a television crew from Tokyo," he explained. "They are doing a segment for a weekly program that covers different topics. This time it's about Isabella Bird's visit to Japan and how she discovered the Ainu on Hokkaido." He smiled. "They have photographs of her they are going to use."

The day I arrived in Shiraoi to follow Isabella Bird's footsteps, she was about to appear on television in Japan for the first time! It seemed a fitting event to mark both our travels. As I left, the museum director promised to send me a videotape of the program. I looked forward to opening the package in Colorado and watching Ainu village life in Shiraoi and Isabella Bird on the very day I visited.

Chapter 11
Noboribetsu
is Hell

I put my arm down several deep crevices and had to withdraw it at once, owing to the great heat. I came to a hot spring, hot enough to burst one of my thermometers, which was above the boiling point of Fahrenheit; and tying up an egg in a pocket handkerchief and holding it by a stick in the water, it was hard boiled in 8½ minutes.

Isabella Bird, Hokkaido, 1878

Noboribetsu is perhaps the most popular hot-spring resort in Hokkaido with an array of brutally ugly hotels and at least eleven different types of hot spring water to soothe ailments or simply invigorate. It is also Japan's most productive hot spring source, churning out some 10,000 tons of piping hot water daily.

Japan Guide, *Lonely Planet,*
1997

Noboribetsu is promoted today as the "hot springs capital of Asia" and "the town built over Hell." A giant statue of a devil looms over the main road into town, and huge, garish devil statues painted red and blue stand on street corners.

A local legend says that a beautiful girl who was very ill begged the King of Hell for help. He told her to soak in the waters of Noboribetsu hot springs, which she did, and was cured. But she had fallen in love with the King of Hell. He rejected her so she plunged into a lake and turned into a blue snake. Once a year in August, the King lifts the cover of Hell, and the two are united. To celebrate, hundreds of people dressed as red and blue demons parade through the streets as goodwill ambassadors appointed by the King. Some pull portable shrines with towering figures of devils and demons, while drummers and dancers provide entertainment. A chillier February celebration includes a hot-water throwing contest between young men in loincloths.

Hot springs and bathing in hot water have been part of Japanese culture for centuries. Noboribetsu's first inn was established in 1858, and the town has been expanding ever since. Today the streets are lined with hotels, resorts, and inns as well as restaurants, souvenir stores, and gift shops.

A taxi took me up the steep, winding mountain road to the family-owned hot springs inn a few miles west of the town where I was to stay. There was no dining room, lounge, or public areas for guests apart from the lobby where I took off my shoes and put on the slippers provided. I was shown to a pleasant room with windows overlooking the garden. There was a television, a couple of low coffee tables, several cushions to sit on, and a futon, quilts, and pillows in the closet to be taken out later. The owner and his wife prepared excellent meals which were served in my room on the low tables at appointed times.

Down the corridor was a steaming indoor hot pool for women, with a counter, mirrors, and stools to wash before soaking. Two women in the water nodded to me when I peeked in. I went out through the glass door to see the small rock-lined pool in the garden, with a bamboo fence separating it from the men's side. Guests come to relax in their rooms and enjoy the hot baths, and often wear the traditional long blue *yukata* robes and slippers all day, even when they take a stroll outside.

When Isabella Bird explored the area she recognized that, as well as hot springs, there were volcanoes in the region. She managed, with difficulty, to scramble to the top of an extinct volcanic cone, and peered into "a deep, well-defined crater of great depth, with its sides richly clothed with vegetation, closely resembling some of the old cones on the island of Kauai."

Today, in Hokkaido's Shikotsu-Toya National Park, like Yellowstone National Park in Wyoming, countless hot springs and steam fumaroles spew up as a result of underground volcanic activity. As I walked along a path in Hell Valley, huge plumes of smoke and thick steam erupted into the air in front of me. A walkway wound over puffing holes and boiling vents to a viewing area. As I stood on the wooden platform, I looked down to watch hot steam pouring out from beneath my feet. Spectacular bursts of steam floated from the rocky slopes, and there was a smell of sulphur in the air. The desolate region of jagged rocks and gravel slopes looked like photographs of the surface of the moon, while the sun struggled to shine eerily through the haze.

I followed a winding trail in the park to the top of a ridge. Below lay a circular crater filled with a vast lake of rippling green water. Rugged gray and white cliffs loomed round the far shores, where bubbling fountains of water erupted from the surface, spurted upwards into the air, and crashed down into the boiling liquid to create a thick plume of rising steam. The noise of water crashing echoed from the cliffs and across the lake. From the surface, bubbling jets rose in puffy white clouds of steam. From the top of the cliffs, thin plumes of steam escaped into the air to float thin and white against the blue sky. The scene changed constantly, and the colors of the blue water and the white steam against the stark cliffs were dramatic.

The area, however, is no longer deserted wilderness. The park is always full of visitors, even on a weekday in October. Couples young and old walked along the paths, taking photographs and videos. Parents pushed children in strollers or carried them in backpacks. A group of older women and men strolled past slowly with sticks. A school group of fifteen small boys neatly dressed in navy uniforms trotted in line after their teacher, who carried a large backpack. As I looked out over the foaming lake, a couple with a teenage son hiked up. The father pointed his camera at the view and tried to pose his wife and son in front of it, but the boy grumbled, "It looked better from the car," and would not smile.

It rained again as Isabella Bird traveled on. She complained that at midnight, "my bed and bedding are so wet that I am still drying them, patch by patch, with tedious slowness, on a wooden frame placed over a charcoal brazier."

Today, people come to Noboribetsu to get wet. In the hundreds of hotels, motels, and hot spring inns, people spend hours soaking in the waters. After a couple of days enjoying the hot bath at my hotel, I went to see Dai-Ichi Takimoto-kan, a luxury hotel renowned for its variety of different baths. It was an overwhelming water experience, a Japanese hot spring heaven.

From the spacious women's changing area, which boasted a bar, sofas and armchairs on one side, and long mirrors, counters, hair dryers, and stools along the other, tall glass doors led into a palatial hall. A line of basins, mirrors, stools, and counters with soap, shampoo, and other creams stood by the door. In the central area, tall columns soared to a high ceiling where natural light flooded in through skylights. A row of ceiling-high windows along one side overlooked a wooded slope. The walls were painted white. White tiles covered the floors.

On every side were streams and pools and jets and baths and sprays of various temperatures. I could hear falling water everywhere, splashing and dripping. I sat on a wooden block under four fierce jets of water from the ceiling, a water massage for shoulders and back that thundered down fiercely. It was too much for me, so I recuperated by slipping into a shallow pool of cool water next to the steam room. It stood beside the wooden sauna room with a pool of truly ice-cold water beside it.

There were whirlpools and gurgling bubble baths and shallow pools, ranging from cool to warm to tepid to hot to boiling. I walked through as many as I could, floating in some, rinsing off in others, feeling the change from hot to warm to cool to cold. In the center, a flight of wide marble steps led up to a vast octagonal pool with steaming hot water. Just below was a long narrow pool with cooler water, covered by a wooden gazebo and surrounded with a wide, tiled shelf for lazing and relaxing. I splashed through the octagon, rinsed off in the narrow pool, and lay on the tiles, feeling relaxed in the steamy, humid air.

Nearby, in a clear blue shallow pool, a mother, grandmother, and a child of about two were sitting and splashing. The two women laughed at the baby's reaction to the water and splashed her. In another pool, three naked women lay contentedly in the water, talking together, while a friend stretched out along the tiled side, occasionally raising her head to join in the conversation. A uniformed woman mopping the floors never gave them a glance.

A sign pointed to an outside pool. I pushed open the heavy doors and found the pool was set amid rocks in a corner sheltered by two sides of the building. On the slope opposite was a thickly planted garden of green shrubs and trees. I walked down the steps and slipped into the pale, misty turquoise water. The air was cool and fresh on my face as I floated in the warm liquid. I gazed up at the blue sky, at the dark red leaves of the Japanese red maple on the slope, at the tiny orange berries on the pyracantha, at the dark green fir trees with their black trunks, and the pale sun flickering through the branches. I had a wonderful feeling of freedom at being alone, outdoors, soaking in warm water, with the sky above, a view of trees, a sense of peace.

Though Isabella Bird longed to stay for another six weeks and explore, it was time for her to go back. On her last morning, she found "the deep blue sky was perfectly unclouded, and the pink summit of the volcano rose into a softening veil of tender blue haze. There was a balmy breeziness in the air, and tawny tints upon the hill, patches of gold in the woods, and a scarlet spray here and there heralded the glories of the advancing autumn."

With her guide, she set off for Hakodate. As she rode through the dense forests, a trailing vine caught her neck. She fell off her horse, and was jammed between a tree trunk and her horse's leg. Her guide rescued her. Later, she looked in a mirror and saw "not only scratches and abrasion all over my face, but a livid mark around my throat as if I had been hung!"

It took her several days traveling by horse, *kurama*, on foot, and by boat to reach Hakodate. When she finally arrived at the British Consulate, she tried to sneak in unobtrusively, "for my old hat, torn green paper waterproof, and my riding-skirt and boots were not only splashed and caked with mud, but I had the general look of a person fresh from the wilds."

She planned to rest and then take a ferry from Hakodate south to Yokohama, which would take about two days by sea, far quicker than her long journey by land.

On my last morning in Noboribetsu, I set out for a walk from my hotel in the mountains, just as the sun was rising, on a perfect fall day. On the horizon stood one sharp volcanic peak and a range of low hills against the pale blue sky. Tall feathery grasses rustled in the breeze amid wildflowers and healthy looking weeds. The trees had touches of red and gold and brown where the leaves were beginning to turn. I strolled along a country road. The path ended at a cliff top, with a view of green fields, wildflowers, and the distant hills, a reminder of what had once been wilderness. As I walked back, I saw a small red fox sunning himself in the grass at the side of the road.

I was ready to journey on. Unlike Isabella Bird, I did not have to return to Hakodate or the British Consulate. Instead, clean and dry, with luggage, map and guidebook in hand, I was now able to do what she could not. I would explore more of Hokkaido before returning to Yokohama.

Chapter 12
Bicycling round Hokkaido

This is really Paradise. Everything is here—huge headlands magnificently timbered, small, deep bays into which the great green waves roll majestically, great gray cliffs too perpendicular for even the most adventurous trailer to find a roothold, inland ranges of mountains forest-covered, with tremendous gorges between, where wolf, bear, and deer make their nearly inaccessible lairs. There seemed no limit to the forest-covered mountains and the unlighted ravines.

Isabella Bird on Hokkaido, 1878

Twenty-five years ago, Japan's systematic environmental destruction was already becoming visible, but there was virtually no popular resistance or dialogue regarding the matter. This destruction has continued at an ever-increasing rate, and now Japan has achieved a position as one of the world's ugliest countries. My friends from abroad who come to visit are almost universally disappointed.

Lost Japan, *Alex Kerr, Lonely Planet Publications, 1996*

W hen Isabella Bird traveled on Hokkaido on horseback, she noticed the effects of the 1868 Japanese govern ment policy of encouraging Japanese from the mainland to move to Hokkaido and establish farms. Near Mori she saw: "The houses are rather plentifully sprinkled along many parts of the shore, and a wonderful profusion of vegetables and flowers about them, raised from seeds liberally supplied by the Katiakushi Department from its Nanai experimental farm and nurseries."

The first settlers were followed by hundreds more during the early 1900s, and after 1945 and the Second World War, thousands more came. Today, Hokkaido is a mix of agricultural lands and farm villages, bustling cities like Sapporo and Asahikawa surrounded by suburban sprawl with more than half of the island's five million population, and areas of untouched wilderness preserved in seven national parks. Visitors come to see the last remnants of the untouched scenery that Isabella Bird admired, with volcanoes, forests, caldera lakes, mountains, wetlands, oceanic islands, and beaches, as well as a few Ainu villages, and enjoy camping, hiking, skiing, climbing, and bus tours around the parks.

Isabella Bird met some of the first Japanese settlers in 1878 when she stayed at an old farmhouse. "A Japanese man and his son are placed here to look after Government interests, and have lived for ten years among the Ainu, and speak their language. They say that the Ainu are thoroughly honest and harmless."

A few houses from early Japanese settlements still dot the rural landscape of Hokkaido. I stayed in a rambling old farmhouse in the farmlands south of Sapporo that had once been a temple; it is now a bed and breakfast run by two enterprising young women, Melissa, an English potter, and Suki, a Japanese weaver and artist. The large main rooms have been converted into studios and an art gallery. We all shared the cozy sitting room with a sofa, armchairs, and a wood-burning stove next to the sunny kitchen. There was also a formal *tatami* mat room, a bathroom with basin, shower, and flush toilet, and a washing machine.

My bedroom had white walls and ceiling. Big windows over-looked a quiet garden. The wooden floor gleamed in parquet squares. A futon lay on either side of the room, with thick quilts covered in a bright floral fabric. A round white paper moon lampshade disguised the ceiling light, and on one wall hung an imposing print of a Japanese woman wrapped in a gray and black robe.

Suki and Melissa provided a mix of Japanese and Western meals. Breakfast, served in the kitchen, was a do-it-yourself affair of tea or coffee, juice, fruit, toast, and cereal. In the evening, they served a Japanese meal in the livingroom round a low table, and we talked about everything under the sun. Melissa had studied pottery in Japan for several years and was preparing for a show. Suki was experimenting with art work in felt and fabrics, which she displayed in the gallery. Both of them had traveled extensively.

On my first morning, I set off on Melissa's bicycle to see what had happened to Hokkaido's once impenetrable wilderness. As I cycled away from the farmhouse along a flat, smooth road to the village of Yuni, there were only a few cars and trucks. I saw a tractor being driven methodically up and down a field, cutting wheat into bundles, and leaving them in lines on the ground. A truck over-loaded with bales waited in a courtyard by a rickety gray, wooden barn. Other fields stretched brown and empty, waiting for the snows of winter. Wild sunflowers at the roadside turned their faces to the sun, just as they do in Colorado. Drab two-storey houses in gray and beige and brown sat behind bushes and trees. In a garden, a woman wearing a traditional farm woman's hat—a wide-brimmed bonnet in a bright flowered fabric that covered her neck—weeded a flower bed. Pink cosmos, orange marigolds, purple dahlias, and sunflowers in bright gold and lemon still bloomed, splashes of color among the green.

I turned off the main road down the hill into Yuni. The narrow streets were quiet, and I easily found the tiny *soba* noodle shop that Suki had recommended. It had half a dozen empty tables, and I ordered *soba* and tea.

I cycled through the town, past a small park with benches and green lawns, and down the road. As I cycled by a group of children walking home from school, they called "Hello" and waved. I pedaled along quiet roads lined with neatly kept houses alongside a canal. At the end of the road, a long flight of steps led to a temple, and I walked up to admire the sculpture of a horse in front. The temple's facade was lined with windows, but the door was locked. I wandered down the path to the graveyard. Among the crowded gravestones was a row of *Jizo*, small statues draped with red and white clothes, the patron saints of children, an odd contrast of gray stone and bright fabrics.

The wilderness that once covered the area had turned into a typical Japanese village. As I bicycled back to the main road, I passed a building site with bulldozers and machinery. On a large board at the front was a drawing of an extensive housing development. I wondered how long the rolling farmlands would be preserved in the face of development. In Colorado, I had watched acres of ranchlands suddenly disappear to become a new city of houses and apartments, squeezed next to each other by the hundreds.

I realized that Hokkaido faced the same problems as many untouched places in the world. The once pristine island now faced pollution, environmental hazards, and danger from its nuclear power plants. It was no longer isolated, and indeed, it was as easy to fax my office in Colorado from here as from anywhere else. Locally grown foods and other products had competition from imports from around the world. And traditional society was being challenged by a demand from women for a new role in a society dominated by men.

Isabella Bird learned a little about Japanese women on her travels. She admired the sturdy farm women who led her horse on the road, watched women working in the fields, talked to the Ainu women, and observed Japanese women in traditional dresses, which she thought confining.

She would have enjoyed the discussion we had one evening with Mika, a friend of Suki's, when we ate *nabe*, a rich stew of fish, chicken, and dozens of different vegetables. We sat on cushions in the *tatami* room around a tablecloth filled with serving bowls of different sizes, and helped ourselves to rice and stew, talking as we ate from our bowls with chopsticks, nibbled pickled plums, and sipped glasses of sake.

Mika, a potter, had been married and divorced, and now lived on her own, a very unusual state in Japan. She looked round at us thoughtfully: "I will tell you what Japanese society is like today for women," she said, and she held her hands close together as if praying. "It is narrow and conservative. There is no place for single women in Japanese society. You marry young and have children. When you're over twenty-six, they don't want you. Married women cannot work—they don't want them in the offices. They want them to have children and stay at home."

Suki is another unusual woman. Her parents live on Hokkaido, and she has a married sister with three children. But Suki prefers to live on her own away from her family. She said: "It is hard. My parents want me to marry, but I am really too old now that I am thirty, and that is a sign of failure. But I don't want to go back home."

Mika expressed her disapproval of the Japanese government's policy of refusing to approve the sale of birth-control pills in Japan. Condoms are the most commonly used form of birth control, and women have frequent legal abortions.

Melissa added her criticisms of the Japanese medical profession. When she went for a check-up, she was instructed to cover her face during the examination, and not speak to the doctor. When she told her Japanese friends about it, they thought there was nothing wrong because "the women treat their doctors as gods and never ever ask them any questions!"

She added: "Foreign women have a hard time here. Japanese men don't take foreign women seriously—they know they will never marry an outsider." One friend had gone out with a Japanese man for two years, and, even though he was a student living at home, he never told his parents because he knew they would be shocked.

Annette looked back at the time she lived in Japan, and said: "Foreign men have a great time here. Any American or British or Australian man will find a girlfriend here, no matter what he looks like or what a dork he is. Now that says something about Japanese men!"

They all laughed.

Listening to the conversation, I realized that Japanese women today faced the same kind of obstacles that Isabella Bird faced in nineteenth century England. Today, Japanese women can attend schools and universities, but for the woman astronaut who went on the shuttle flight with John Glenn, or the women athletes who qualify for the Olympics, they must possess enormous dedication and struggle to reach their goals and to achieve such eminence in their fields. Japanese girls and women face enormous social pressure to do what is acceptable, just as Isabella Bird did a century ago. A Japanese woman who lives independently and does not marry, or becomes an artist, a scientist, a doctor, a politician, or a travel author, must have unquenchable faith, determination, courage, and strength.

In the 1850s, Isabella Bird's only option was to marry, have children, and be dependent on her husband. Because she knew she could earn money by writing articles, she decided to lead an independent life. She and her sister chose to live together in Scotland. Isabella supported them with her travel writing, and her sister looked after the house. At the age of fifty, after her sister tragically died, she married a doctor, with an agreement that he would not stop her traveling. When he died five years later, she set off on some of her most adventurous trips to Persia, China, and Turkey and wrote her most impressive books and articles.

In 1892, she was honored as the first woman Fellow of the Royal Geographical Society. But a year later, protests by male members banned more women from being admitted. She commented: "The proposed action is a dastardly injustice to women." Throughout her life, she determinedly struggled to live independently and be recognized for her achievements as a woman. I realized that Isabella Bird would have felt remarkably at home in modern Japan!

Her travels were almost over. She spent her last days in Hakodate clearing up her affairs and said goodbye to Ito, who told her he was sorry that it was the last morning. She wrote: "I was indeed very sorry to end my pleasant tour. I have parted with Ito finally today, with great regret. He has served me faithfully. He insisted on packing for me as usual, and put all my things in order."

The ferry Isabella Bird boarded in Hakodate harbor was supposed to take two days to reach Yokohama. But a typhoon struck. Giant waves rocked the boat, the captain was forced to jettison the cargo, and Isabella Bird languished in her cabin. When she reached the harbor a day late, she found floods and storms had caused much damage to the city, and she went to rest at her hotel.

Melissa drove me to Sapporo to catch the train south on my last day on Hokkaido and gave me detailed instructions on how to change trains for Yokohama. I had a couple of hours to spare so I walked over to the Hokkaido University Botanical Gardens. Set behind iron railings and surrounded by tall office buildings, it had thousands of local and imported plants, many of which Isabella Bird saw growing in their natural habitat. I sat on the carefully manicured, soft, green lawn, surrounded by tall cherry trees and feathery bamboo plants. A Japanese couple were talking together on a bench, a woman read a book under a tree, a man in a business suit was stretched out asleep. The sounds of police sirens whined through the air above the growl of traffic.

I looked back at the long chain of events that had brought me here, from Isabella Bird's trip to Japan "for her health" and my fascination with travel and writing that led me to her Colorado book, and her Japan book that had inspired my trip here. I had always admired her courage in deciding to spend her life traveling instead of conforming to the rules of a narrow Victorian society. I understood how alike we both were in our unquenchable passion to travel to new places and explore distant lands. I would love to have been able to tell her that her name and her book were still remembered in Japan, and what fun it had been to follow her footsteps.

As I walked out of the park, I noticed a sign pointing to an Ainu Museum. It was housed in an old redbrick Victorian building with objects displayed in glass cases in plain square rooms. I strolled past the Ainu artifacts I now recognized—sake bowls, decorated sticks, woven garments, spears, fish hooks, dug out canoes—and photographs of villages with their straw huts and bear cages. I wandered into the museum store. There, among the postcards and souvenirs, was the cover of a book I now knew very well, the Japanese translation of Isabella Bird's *Unbeaten Tracks in Japan.*

I left Sapporo on a Japanese bullet train that zipped through the undersea tunnel and across the countryside at record speed. We arrived on time. I took a taxi to my hotel on the waterfront to find that my room overlooked the harbor where Isabella's ferryboat had finally arrived.

Chapter 13
Yokohama

The journey between Yokohama and Tokyo is performed in an hour by an admirable, well-metaled, double-track railroad, 18 miles long, with iron bridges, neat stations, and substantial roomy termini built by English engineers at a cost known only to the Government, and opened by the Mikado in 1872. The Yokohama Station is a handsome and suitable stone building.

Isabella Bird, 1878

Except during Tokyo's rush-hour madness, trains in Japan are delightful and obsessively punctual. Japan is a nation where train travel undertaken for its own sake is a highly-regarded popular pastime. Trains come in diverse configurations, from rustic simplicity to glossy sleepers intended for honeymoon flirtations to the so-called "bullet train" or *shinkansen* running at silky-smooth high speed, and charging fares to match its velocity.

On the Move in Japan, *Scott Rutherford, Yen Books, 1995*

Isabella Bird's stay in Yokohama did not please her. She thought the city "has a dead-alive look. It has irregularity without picturesqueness, and the gray sky, gray sea, gray houses, and gray roofs look harmoniously dull." She stayed in a hotel near the British Consulate. The hotel was run by a Frenchman who "relies on a Chinaman, the servants are Japanese boys in Japanese clothes, and there is a Japanese groom of the chambers in faultless English costume, who perfectly appalls me by the elaborate politeness of his manner."

From her window she observed "heavy, two-wheeled man-carts drawn and pushed by four men each, on which nearly all goods are carried. Ladies drive themselves about the town in small pony carriages attended by running grooms. The foreign merchants keep carts pulled by coolies constantly standing at their doors." She saw the harbor waters filled with thousands of fishing boats, "their hulls being unpainted wood, and their sails pure white duck. Now and then a high-sterned junk drifted by like a phantom galley, and a fleet of triangular-looking fishing boats with white square sails."

I liked Yokohama, the mix of people, the ocean, the ships on the water, and the bustle of the waterfront. I stayed in the newly opened Pan Pacific Hotel, a skyscraper on the bay, part of the ambitious development program for the area. In the hotel were elegant French, Italian, Chinese, and Japanese restaurants, places for drinks, snacks, coffee or tea, and superb room service. The Japanese staff was unfailingly polite and helpful. My room was tastefully furnished with armchairs, desk, soft beige carpeting, and color television. The luxurious bathroom had a soft, heated toilet seat, massage sprays in the shower, and a bath placed so I could look out at the bay while I soaked and admired the curving arc of the Yokohama Bay suspension bridge, cruise liners and oil tankers anchored in the distance, sightseeing boats and marine shuttles churning across the water, and fishing boats speeding across the ripples.

Yokohama is now Japan's second largest city, with a population of more than three million people. In the Maritime Museum I wandered past photographs and displays that showed the city's growth from a small fishing village to its present importance as a major port. The original port was devastated by the 1923 earthquake and then rebuilt and modernized over the years. Today, more than 126 million tons of cargo and more than 50,000 vessels come into the port each year. Outside, moored at the wharf, was a restored three-masted schooner with white sails and gleaming brass and wood fittings, one of the last sailing vessels in service in the 1930s, and now used as a training ship by the navy.

A model of the old city in the Kanagawa Museum of Cultural History shows the original wooden buildings—city hall, private houses, shops, the British Consulate—along tree-lined streets. Today, the Consulate is the home of the Yokohama Archives of History. An imposing entrance leads into a courtyard surrounded by gray stone buildings. Inside are displays of old costumes, photos, and maps. I looked through bound copies of the English language newspaper, *The Japan Gazette*, and found "Miss Bird" listed in an October 16, 1878 issue under "Arrivals," the day she arrived back from Hokkaido.

As her departure drew closer, Isabella Bird found "the time has flown by in excursions, shopping, select little dinner parties, farewell calls." Though she was noteworthy enough to be listed in the paper, she did not impress everyone favorably. Clara A. N. Whitney, a young American girl, met her at a Christian Association social and wrote in her diary: "Lady Parkes could not go, but sent instead a very disagreeable old maid, Miss Isabella Bird, who is going to write a book. She pumps everybody until everyone hates to go near her."

In my last two days, I explored the city of Yokohama. My first local guide, yet another Mr. Ito, was a lively, energetic, retired English teacher who had been an exchange teacher in Portland, Maine, and in the Czech Republic. He arrived with leaflets and an audiotape about Yokohama for me so that I would know what there was to see. I told him

I had studied my guidebooks and knew where I wanted to go. He looked dubious, but I explained my proposed itinerary, and he nodded cheerfully.

"*Hai, hai, hai!* We walk, because that is the best way to see everything." With his video camera at the ready, we set off at a brisk pace.

He was full of information and stories, and yet relaxed enough to let me linger and look at what interested me. When Isabella Bird traveled through the farm communities of the north, she visited a factory of handloom silk-weavers with 180 employees, half of them women, and noted: "These new industrial openings for respectable employment for women and girls are very important, and tend in the direction of much-needed social reform." I visited the silk museum, where beautiful old Japanese robes and dresses as well as hangings, wraps, and doll clothes were displayed together with modern scarves and clothes. Silk-weaving techniques date back to the fifteenth century in Japan when silk clothes were adopted by the samurai and spread throughout the country. Isabella Bird saw silkworms being raised in farmhouses, and local women spinning silk threads on their looms.

At lunchtime, Mr. Ito knew exactly where to go. We marched through the winding streets of Chinatown, which is one of the largest in the world, to his favorite restaurant. There was a large Chinese population in Yokohama when Isabella Bird visited: "Of the 2,500 Chinamen who reside in Japan, over 1,100 are in Yokohama, and if they were suddenly removed, business would come to an abrupt halt. Here, as everywhere, the Chinese immigrant is making himself indispensable. He walks through the streets with his swinging gait and air of complete self-complacency, as though he belonged to the ruling race."

Today, thronged with people, and filled with color, noise, and activity, Chinatown is one of the liveliest places in Yokohama. Four curving gates, painted in vivid red and gold, bridge the main streets guarding north, south, east, and west. Talkative crowds stroll past storefront windows offering sweets, baked good, meat buns, cooking ingredients, clothing, arts and crafts, and Chinese tea. Hundreds of restaurants offer dishes from different regions of China. The noise and color are a sharp contrast to the bleak modern skyscrapers of the new waterfront and the drab buildings of the old Yokohama.

Mr. Ito's favorite restaurant was on a side street. We walked up its narrow stairs to be seated at a table next to a noisy group of businessmen and had egg rolls, hot and sour soup, chicken with lemon, fried rice, and hot tea. From there, we walked—slightly less briskly!—to Yamashita Park on the waterfront. Looking out over the bay with a constantly changing view of ships, the park is a favorite place for visitors and residents. Couples, families, and people who work in city offices strolled along the waterfront promenade lined with trees and benches. Mr. Ito showed me a charming statue of a little girl, "The Girl with Red Shoes," famous in a popular children's song. He sang the song from sheet music which he had specially copied for me. A Japanese couple standing beside us were intrigued, asked him innumerable questions, nodding sagely as he told them everything he knew, and they clapped after he sang the song again.

"Now I will show you where to get the least expensive cup of coffee in Yokohama," said Mr. Ito. Seeing my doubtful expression, he added: "It is excellent coffee."

We took a ferry and bounced across the water to the new development near my hotel. I followed him over a wide plaza and through tall glass doors into Queens Court, a brand new shopping mall. I have lived in New Jersey, the kingdom of the malls, and have visited dozens of malls in the United States. Unbelievably, this was one of the most lavish, extravagant, ornate, and affluent malls I have ever seen anywhere.

There were several floors linked by escalators, and every floor was lined with the spotless glass windows of fancy stores filled with high-priced merchandise, designed for those for whom joy is shopping. The size, variety of stores, space, display, and price took my breath away. In the glittering Time-Warner store, selling all manner of Disney merchandise, I picked up a Bugs Bunny doll and noticed it was made in China. I spotted L. L. Bean, Eddie Bauer, Tiffany's, The Body Shop, and dozens more stores whose names are household words in America, France, Japan, and England. Flashy souvenir stores, electronic stores, and pachinko games stores were next to window after window after window filled with china plates, silver knives, dried flower arrangements, fresh flowers, chocolates, blue jeans, silk scarves, sweaters, jewelry, shoes, make-up, and more.

Along the wide marbled walkways strolled hundreds of people shopping—men and women of all ages and nationalities, schoolgirls in uniform, teenagers in thick-heeled shoes and short skirts, women with children, young couples, old women together. It was my first exposure to the modern, commercial, fast-paced materialistic side of Japan that I had tried to avoid, and it was astonishing.

Mr. Ito led me downstairs to a lower level, where there were scores of restaurants and snack bars including the Hard Rock Café, Kentucky Fried Chicken, Mister Donut, and Starbucks. In a food court under a department store I saw cakes, chocolates, meringues, desserts, fresh bread, and cookies beautifully displayed. Farther along was a vast assortment of ready-to-eat foods as well as fresh fruit, vegetables, meat and fish. At a counter, a woman wrapped a box of truffles in patterned silver paper and tied it with ribbon. I was amazed by the affluence, the buying, the products, the packaging, the sheer extravagance of it all.

Mr. Ito did not waver from his mission to show me where to find the cheapest cup of coffee in Yokohama. I followed him into a coffee bar packed with people at a central counter and at tables. I perched on a stool while he bought coffee for both of us. It may have been inexpensive, but it was strong, tasty, and fresh. We sat sipping it and talked about Isabella Bird, how I had discovered her, and where I had been. Then he told me about all the wonderful places near here I had to see. I said I'd come back and he could show me around. He was still full of energy and enthusiasm. It had been a really interesting day. He led me along a corridor to an inconspicuous door that led into the lobby of my hotel. I thanked him profusely and went to have a rest.

My next guide was an economist, with a pessimistic view on life. Mr. Miserable Ito, as I nicknamed him, was a solid, square man with thin lips, round red cheeks, and thinning black hair. As we walked past the new skyscrapers along the waterfront, he grumbled: "This is a terrible time. The economy here will collapse, and these will soon be empty, because the rents are too high, and there is no financing to complete them." I said that I hadn't seen much evidence of poverty or economic disaster, but he shook his head: "It is going to end, the economy is failing here, and it will spread around the world. There will be a total collapse."

He didn't seem particularly interested in the places I wanted to see, told me it wasn't worth trying to drive to nearby historic gardens because the traffic would be too heavy, and, after wandering around a couple of museums, we went to lunch. The place he liked was in the mall. I followed him to an Italian restaurant. Sitting on high stools at a counter, I crunched my Japanese pizza with a very thin crust and fresh vegetables and grated seaweed on top. He had spaghetti with grated seaweed and fish eggs, and a soft drink. The cappuccino was excellent.

He needed to buy a book from the bookstore in the mall so we went up the escalators to the top floor. There I discovered Yurindo, a huge English language bookstore. It was heaven! I was surrounded by thousands of books in English for the first time since I left Colorado. When Mr. Ito came back with his book, still looking dour, I realized I had no desire to spend any more time sightseeing with someone so depressing. I explained I loved the bookstore and would stay here. He looked surprised but said nothing. We shook hands, bowed, and he left me in my favorite place.

When I finally tore myself away, it was late. I walked back through the mall to the hotel. As I turned a corner, I found a crowd of people cheering as they watched a wall-size TV screen. The Yokohama Baystars baseball team was fighting for a place in the finals of the Japanese Central League. Everyone clapped in rhythm with the stadium crowds and rooted for the home team. I stood by a pillar, with a pang of nostalgia for Coors Field where I've watched the Colorado Rockies on a blue sky summer day, for the Red Sox in Fenway Park where I used to go, and for the summer evenings I've sat in front of the TV counting pitches and strikes, hits and runs. I knew exactly what was going on, and the Yokohama Baystars won!

The next morning, feeling perfectly confident about sightseeing on my own without a guide, I spent my last day visiting the Museum of Art, which had an exhibit of American pop art, and strolling along the waterfront. I sat on a wide stone step facing the water. Motorboats bounced over the ripples, seagulls wheeled above, the mournful horn of a steamer echoed over the water. Nearby, two young women sat reading, their dark hair flopping over their faces. A mother pushed an empty stroller as her little boy toddled ahead, and she hurried to keep up with him. A schoolgirl in an extremely short skirt and white socks held hands with a schoolboy in uniform. A young woman clunked past in high black suede boots with thick heels, wearing black tights, a thigh-high skirt, and a black military jacket. A man carrying a dustpan and broom walked slowly along the wide steps, sweeping up cigarette butts and scraps of paper.

I felt part of the scenery, no longer a stranger. I could understand what was happening, and I knew how to behave. I could even speak a few words of Japanese. I listened to the slaps of water against the stone quay, the voices of people walking past, a boat sounding its horn before it left, a plane droning overhead, colorful flags flapping on a pole, the faint music from the restaurant on the quay, the sounds of a child laughing, the booming of a loudspeaker announcing the departure of the next ferryboat.

It was time to leave Japan. "I have spent the last ten days here, in settled fine weather, such as should have begun two months ago if the climate behaved as it ought," noted Isabella Bird. She packed her boxes, left behind what she no longer needed, and took the new train, which had been built by British engineers, from Tokyo to Yokohama. On the way, she observed: "The immediate neighborhood of Yokohama is beautiful, with abrupt wooded hills, and small picturesque valleys. Every foot of land which can be seen from the railroad is cultivated by the most careful spade husbandry, and much of it is irrigated for rice. Streams abound, and villages of gray wooden houses with gray thatch, and gray temples with strangely curved roofs, are scattered thickly over the landscape. It is all homelike, liveable, and pretty, the country of an industrious people, for not a weed is to be seen."

I took the bus from the Yokohama airline terminal near the hotel to Tokyo's Narita Airport. The scenery was depressingly different from what Isabella Bird described. After we crossed the Yokohama Bay Bridge, the bus turned onto modern highways edged with dingy gray and brown warehouses, glassy office buildings, black-topped parking lots, huge stacks of containerized boxes waiting by railroad lines, and gray apartment buildings like gigantic shoe boxes with rows of metal balconies. It looked like the New Jersey Turnpike in rush hour. Cars growled nose to nose along the rain-slicked roadway, lumbering trucks oozed by steadily, and the bus passengers sat morosely staring or sleeping as the minutes dragged by. Outside, rain dripped down the windows.

Before Isabella Bird left for England, she was interviewed by a daily newspaper, the *Yomi-uri-Shimbun*. It had, she commented pompously, "the largest, though not the most aristocratic, circulation in Tokyo, being taken by servants and tradespeople." The paper gave a "very inaccurate but entertaining account" of her expedition, noting: "This lady spends her time in traveling, leaving this year the two American continents for a passing visit to the Sandwich Islands, and landing in Japan early in the month of May. She toured all over the country, and even made a five months stay in Hokkaido, investigating the local customs and productions."

Before I flew back to the United States, I was interviewed by Kelly Langpap, a reporter on Tokyo's *Asahi Evening News* of the Asahi Shimbun company. Her editor assigned her to interview me in Yokohama after hearing about my journey from an American travel news publication. The long newspaper article about Isabella Bird's visit and my travels concluded:

"Both women are impressive not only for their adventurousness and insight, but their eagerness to introduce others to some of the weirdness and wonderfulness of other places and cultures. And then there's the fact they have made a living doing it. Kaye acknowledges that the freedom she has enjoyed to go wherever and do whatever she's wanted makes Bird's accomplishments all the more awesome in comparison.

"Looking back on her own trip through Japan, Kaye said she was stunned by the impact that one woman had made on the places she visited. Yamagata has a local history museum with 25 percent of its display space devoted to Isabella Bird, and a quote from her book about an Asian Arcadia was made into the theme for a ten-year plan of beautification and preservation. It goes without saying that their experiences of the country were vastly different. And writers like Bird and Kaye make it possible to have wild adventures without ever having to leave the sofa."

On December 19, 1878, Isabella Bird boarded her steamer. She saw "the snowy dome of Fujisan reddening in the sunrise rose above the violet woodlands as we steamed out of Yokohama Harbor." Three days later, she glimpsed "the last of Japan—a rugged coast, lashed by a wintry sea."

On October 26, 1998, after two hours oozing through the traffic on the bus to the airport. I checked in, had a snack, and sat in the lounge to wait. The rain poured down the windows. It was almost dark outside. I waited again when the boarding announcements began before I filed onto the Japan Airlines plane, and waited for departure. The plane taxied along the shiny runway and, with a roar, swooped up into the night.

I peered out of the window to see millions of lights spread like a giant twinkling carpet, flickering from office buildings and apartment houses, buses and cars, street lamps and traffic lights. As the plane climbed through the clouds, the lights disappeared. It was my last view of Japan.

Chapter 14 Looking Back

In many things, specially in some which lie on the surface, the Japanese are greatly our superiors, but in many others they are immeasurably behind us. In living altogether among this courteous, industrious, and civilized people, one is doing them a gross injustice in comparing their manners and ways with those of a people molded by many centuries of Christianity

Isabella Bird, 1878

The Japanese see themselves largely as Westerners see them—polite, loyal, hard-working, conformist and not profoundly inventive. They also see national characteristics that foreigners often overlook—their high average level of education, their profound sensitivity to nature. And they reverse some commonly-held prejudices, regarding themselves as warm, impulsive, and sentimental, and Westerners as cold, calculating, and unfathomable. Above all they take pride in the fact that they are Japanese—and no one else is.

A Traveller's History of Japan, *Richard Tames, Interlink Books, 1997*

The hand-carved wooden owl from the Ainu woodcarver in Biratori sits on top of my computer looking at me with brown hooded eyes. He's about three inches high, and round, with two neatly carved feet. The piece of wood is dark, with patterned wood circles on top of his head and on his back, while his body and face are light. He reminds me of Biratori and Hokkaido, of the many places I visited and the people I met, and my surprising introduction to the real Japan.

Before I arrived, I expected to feel isolated and confused as I traveled around because I could not read or speak Japanese. I planned to avoid cities and see the rural north, and I knew that fewer people spoke English in smaller communities. I worried that I would experience discrimination because I looked like a *gaijin,* or foreigner. I also worried about being a woman in a society where feminism was not popular and women did not travel alone.

I need not have worried. I was welcomed and accepted because my guides knew about Isabella Bird. I had a personal introduction to the places I visited. One of my Mr. Ito guides took me home to meet his wife and mother; I admired their beautiful Japanese garden with waving grasses, carefully placed rocks, and a pond with fat golden carp swimming. Another asked me if he could introduce his wife to me, and we stopped by his house and talked about Isabella Bird and what I was doing. My Tajima guide invited me to stay with her, where I had an opportunity to meet a Japanese woman who knew all about Miss Bird.

I stayed at small hotels and met the owners, soaked in hot tubs and baths, ate delicious local food—and several excellent Italian meals—

and learned to use my chopsticks like an expert. I went by train and bus, bicycle and on foot, to confirm that Isabella Bird went where she said she had gone, and she is well remembered for having gone there. It proved to be the ideal way to see Japan for the first time, with a nineteenth century lady leading me to places off the beaten track.

When Isabella Bird first saw Japan, the country was emerging from two centuries of isolation; it was a complete contrast to the 1878 England she knew. England was enjoying a booming industrial revolution, had an extensive network of transportation by canal, railway, and road, and had hotels and inns in every town and village for travelers. Though she was critical of much that she found in Japan, she added: "The scenes are strictly representative, and I offer them in the interests of truth, for they illustrate the nature of a large portion of the material with which the Japanese Government has to work in building up the New Civilization."

I had never visited Japan before so nothing prepared me for the intense familiarity that I experienced. To my astonishment, the more I saw of Japan, the more I was reminded of England. Though I have lived in the United States for more than thirty years, my childhood was spent in the suburbs of London in the 1950s, when England was far less diverse and multicultural than it is now. Japan is still a very homogenous place. About 2% of the total population are non-Japanese, including the Ainu. I kept being reminded of the England that I remembered. From the moment I arrived, I recognized dozens of similarities.

Driving: The Japanese drive on the left-hand side of the road, as they do in England. Many roads in Hokkaido and the smaller communities of the north are narrow, two-lane streets winding through the countryside and look just like roads in Essex or Surrey or Devon. Japanese cars and vans are small and compact, like most English automobiles, not like the sprawling American sedans and sport utility vehicles I see on Colorado highways. In addition, the Japanese, like the British, use their bicycles for daily transportation.

Trains: The first train between Yokohama and Tokyo was built by British engineers. Today, Japan's extensive train service is efficient, punctual, and comfortable. England's train service has been reduced, but city railway systems and long-distance trains are widely used to avoid the crowded roads. Both Japanese and English people often travel by train to work, to school, on vacation, to visit family and friends, when Americans automatically drive cars.

Housing: Along the narrow streets of England and Japan are compact, one or two-storey houses, designed to provide just enough space without lavishness, often with plain square windows and brick or stucco on the outside. The suburban sprawl around Sapporo and other northern cities looked like suburban sprawl round English towns. Stores and shops usually have display windows and side-door entrances, and there are only a few low-key supermarkets here and there, unlike the vast, neon-lit American supermarkets. In Japan, the pachinko parlors are often the jazziest looking buildings, with music and noise, flashing neon lights, big windows, and colorful signs.

Gardening: Japanese and English houses have neatly tended gardens where people grow flowers and vegetables, and mow their green lawns. There are some differences, as I saw when I walked round a local bonsai miniature tree exhibit in Hirosaki, where earnest judges discussed the finer points of tiny red maples and pencil-thin oaks. It reminded me of flower shows in England, where dedicated diggers bring in their petunias and roses with quiet pride.

Land: Both Japan and England are island countries with very little space for a large number of people. Unlike the United States, there are no great areas of land still available for sale, or spacious farms, and rolling ranches. Everything is pretty well developed and built up. For that reason, the parks and national forests are often filled at vacation times with crowds of visitors going hiking and camping.

Royalty: Japan has an Emperor and Empress, and England has a Queen and her consort. The long history behind both thrones is filled with vicious bloodshed, battles, murder, and civil wars for power. Schoolchildren learn the gruesome details in history classes and are not perturbed by the violence of the past. In both countries, there have been wars with neighboring countries—China and Korea, France and Germany—though there is now peace.

Rain: Because Japan and England are surrounded by water, it rains throughout the year, and the wetness is part of the culture, except on Hokkaido, which has no rainy season. Both the English and the Japanese automatically take raincoats and umbrellas whenever they go out. It is perpetually about to rain, drizzling, pouring, or it's just stopped raining so everything is wet. The steady year-round moisture keeps the scenery looking beautifully green in both countries. The Japanese and the English stoically accept rain as part of their environment. Outdoor events are rarely canceled because it's wet. Once at an English bed and breakfast, when I was planning to go hiking, rain poured down the windows outside as our waitress served breakfast and said cheerily: "Aren't we lucky with the weather?" In Japan, when I told my Nikko guide that we had been lucky it hadn't rained, he replied: "Everything is still there in the rain."

Cold: The Japanese, like the British, pretend it doesn't really get cold in winter. In Japan, it was cold enough to hold the Winter Olympics in Hokkaido, and the snow often reaches the rooftops. In England, snow blocks roads in the north, dumps several inches in the south, and cold weather freezes water pipes on the outsides of houses. Though weather records show a long history of cold, damp winters in both countries, the Japanese and the British have rejected the American ideal of modern central heating and prefer to use oil heaters, fireplaces or wood stoves, and provide heated toilet seats. The weather is always a major topic of conversation.

Clothes: In Japan and England, people dress more formally than in America, where casual clothes are acceptable almost everywhere. In both countries, there are also recognized societal expectations about what kind of clothes can be worn on different occasions—for the office, to a party, on the street, visiting friends. Both countries expect people to know the rules and wear what is expected. Not wearing the correct outfit is a sign of ignorance.

Politeness: Compared to Americans, the Japanese and the English are always very polite in a formal way. They communicate within a structured etiquette of behavior, and there are certain phrases you are expected to say in a conversational exchange, unlike the American's easy-going "Hi, how are ya?" Learning the rules is difficult, but it eases social contacts because noone wants to offend anyone or make a scene. Foreigners love the politeness, though it's hard to know what people really think.

Tea: The Japanese drink quantities of tea. So do the British. The Japanese offer tea as soon as you arrive, make tea at every opportunity, proffer tea at offices, have teahouses, tea companies, a tradition of artistic teapots, teacups, and tea services on trays, and a history of tea as part of the fabric of society. So do the British. And they both drink coffee, too, which is extremely popular.

Beer: Japanese and British men drink quantities of beer at every opportunity. They have a number of home-brewed beers, meet in bars or pubs to drink beer, entertain friends by drinking beer, and frequently get drunk. This is socially acceptable.

America: Both Japan and England today enjoy an open infatuation with all things American, from movies to music to Coca-Cola to blue jeans. Japan imports American baseball players, while the British are playing American football. Both countries look back to a time when their attitude was different. England's account of America's War of Independence, when the American colony refused to pay taxes, defeated the English army, and proclaimed itself a separate state, is briefly covered in a couple of paragraphs in most modern history books. Japan is inclined to downplay the harrowing events of the Second World War.

School children: Japanese girls and boys travel to and from school on trains and buses in school uniforms, just as schoolchildren do in England. It was astonishing to see the familiar navy and gray and blue blazers and shirts, skirts, and pants on Japanese children. Japanese schools, like English schools, have competitive examinations and tremendous pressure to succeed in order to be accepted at universities and colleges.

Values: In Japan as in England, privilege and status are often more significant than wealth. A noble family and recognized honors are valued more than monetary attributes. In addition, the subtleties of class, personal contacts, and social position are critical for success. Artists, writers, actors, and musicians are also revered. Business has become important in this century, but respected families and successful artists are admired more than millionaires.

Regions: The south is the favored region of the country. The division between the north and the south has many historic, social, political, and economic repercussions. In both countries, there are jokes and stories about the difference between northerners and southerners.

Women: Both countries have men in most positions of power, and women are paid less and are rarely major leaders. In England, women are visible in the workplace, sports world, and in the media. In Japan, after marriage, a woman is expected to stay home and look after the children. In both countries, organizations are working to gain greater opportunities for women.

The more I noticed the similarities between the two countries, the more I thought how surprised British Isabella Bird would have been to find the country she had found so strange now resembled the country of her birth. The longer I traveled, the more grateful I was to be following in her footsteps. She provided me with a unique introduction to the real Japan.

I look at the carved Ainu owl sitting on my computer. I'm sad to say goodbye to Isabella Bird after such a great trip. I wonder if, in 120 years time, another adventurous traveler will set off to follow her footsteps once again.

THANKS AND
ACKNOWLEDGMENTS

Researching and writing this book was an astonishing adventure as I followed Isabella Bird's route through Japan.

Though today's roads and train routes follow much the same paths north, some place names have changed. I have used modern placenames in the book. The only place I didn't manage to visit was Niigata, on the west coast of Honshu, where Isabella Bird went to spend a few days relaxing with English friends at a Church Mission House.

My sincere thanks to Marian Goldberg in the Japan National Tourist Office in New York who was a gold mine of information. Her office provided maps of where Isabella Bird went based on the old placenames, sent a deluge of printed materials, recommended a rail pass, and told me about local Japanese Goodwill Guides who show you round for a day, free of charge, in exchange for lunch.

American guides who specialize in cultural trips to Japan gave me excellent advice, and my sincere thanks especially to Nancy Craft in Colorado, who was a superb guide, and also to David Everhart and Susan Place, Debra Loomis, Steve Beimel, Alice North, and Kate Ohlberg.

David and Chisato Dubreuil are Ainu experts who gave me helpful information about where to go on Hokkaido and sent a great quote about Isabella Bird's visit there. William Fitzhugh of the Smithsonian Institution provided e-mail encouragement and advice.

Colorado has unexpected Japanese connections. My sincere thanks to Masahiro Nobusaka of the Japan External Trade Organization in Denver, the Boulder-Yamagata Sister City group, Susan Schmidt, director of the University of Colorado at Boulder Study Abroad Japan program, and John and Yayoi Shaw. For Japanese names of people, I have used the Japanese form and put the last name first.

In Japan, my thanks to Doreen Simmons, Mary King, and May Leong in Tokyo, who sent e-mail information and suggestions. And many thanks to Molly Cahill, Kelly Langpap, Michelle Dalton Tyree, Janet Gardner, Kate and Leiko, Shaney Crawford, Hiroko Sukarai, Yoko Aoyama, Yoshimi Mizuno, Nozomi Oishi, Toshihiko Sawada, Shigemi Minetaka, Takeshi Kato, Naokoo Kuwaki, Kaziio Miyaska, Yoshie Kira, Erwan LeBras, Eiichi Ito, Toshihide Ito, Takeshi Takeda, Kunihide Komuro, Kumido Ohta, Kikuchi Royoko, Miyuki Muraki, Shigeki Akino, Yoneda Hikeki, Masaki Sonobe, Akiko Ilzuka, Miki Kaneko, Mr. Watanabe, Yomiko Saito, Junicho Kudo, and the dozens of sympathetic people I met who answered my questions in pathetic Japanese and helped me on my way.

My sincere thanks to the people who read the first drafts of the book and gave me their opinions so I could do better, to Molly O'Halloran in Chicago, who was recommended by Amy Mitchell, for her maps, and to Sallie Greenwood, who proofread carefully for all the misplaced commas.

Finally, my love and appreciation to my family in Boulder—David, Lisa, Claire, Spencer, Katrina and Nick—who understand my Itchy-Feet Syndrome, and provide hugs and support along the way; and to my wonderful husband, Christopher Sarson, who hated the idea of my going to Japan on my own, but nobly offered creative suggestions and ideas and once again provided his outstanding literary and computer skills as an editor and designer for the book.

BIBLIOGRAPHY

Books about Japan: Guidebooks

Gateway to Japan, Third Edition (Kodansha International, 1998)
Insight Guides—Tokyo (APA Publications/Houghton Mifflin, 1996)
Japan (Lonely Planet Publications, 1997)

General books

Basho, Matsuo. *Narrow Road to the Interior* (Stone Bridge Press, 1996)
Booth, Alan. *The Roads to Sata: A 2,000 mile walk through Japan* (Viking, 1985)
Brown, Jan. *Exploring Tohuku* (John Weatherhill, 1982)
Busch, Noel F. *The Horizon Concise History of Japan* (American Heritage, 1972)
Chamberlain, Basil Hall. *Japanese Things* (Tuttle, 1971)
Davidson, Kathy N. *36 Views of Mount Fuji: On Finding Myself in Japan* (Plume/Penguin, 1994)
Downer, Lesley. *On the Narrow Road: Journey into a Lost Japan* (Summit Books, 1985)
Gibney, Frank. *Five Gentlemen of Japan: The Portrait of a Nation's Character* (Tuttle, 1954)
Golden, Arthur. *Memoirs of a Geisha* (Vintage Contemporary, 1999)
Iyer, Pico. *The Lady and the Monk: Four Seasons in Kyoto* (Vintage Departures, 1991)

Kayano, Shigeru. *The Romance of the Bear God: Ainu Folktales* (Taishukan, 1985)

Kayano, Shigeru. *Our Land was a Forest* (Westview Press, 1994)

Kaye, Evelyn. *Amazing Traveler: Isabella Bird* (Blue Panda, 1999)

Kerr, Alex. *Lost Japan* (Lonely Planet Journeys, 1996)

Kokichi, Katsu. *Musui's Story: Autobiography of a Tokugawa Samurai* (University of Arizona Press, 1988)

Kriska, Laura. *The Accidental Office Lady* (Tuttle, 1997)

Morley, John David. *Pictures from the Water Trade: Adventures of a Westerner in Japan* (Perennial Library/Atlantic Monthly Press, 1985)

Rutherford, Scott. *On the Move in Japan: Useful Phrases and Common Sense for the Traveler* (Yenbooks, 1996)

Sugimoto, Edsu Inagaki. *Daughter of the Samurai* (Doubleday, Doran & Co., 1934)

Tames, Richard. *A Traveller's History of Japan* (Interlink Books, 1997)

Whitney, Clara A. N. *Clara's Diary: An American girl in Meiji Japan* (Kodansha International, 1979)

Books by Isabella Bird

Unbeaten Tracks in Japan (John Murray,1880; Virago/Beacon Press, 1987)

A Lady's Life in the Rocky Mountains (John Murray,1879: University of Oklahoma Press, 1960)

Hawaii: Six Months among the Palm Groves, Coral Reefs, and Volcanoes of the Sandwich Islands (John Murray,1875; Tuttle, 1974)

The Golden Chersonese (John Murray, 1883; Century Publishing, 1983)

Journeys in Persia and Kurdistan (John Murray, 1891: Virago, 1988)

Among the Tibetans (Religious Tract Society,1894; Revell, 1894)

Korea and Her Neighbors (John Murray,1898; Tuttle,1986)

Yangtze Valley and Beyond (John Murray,1899; Virago/Beacon Press,1987)

TRAVEL RESOURCES

Embassy of Japan

WASHINGTON, D. C.
2520 Massachusetts Avenue NW.
Washington DC 20008

WEB SITE
http://www.embjapan.org/

Japanese Consulates are in the following cities: Agana, Guam; Anchorage, Atlanta, Boston, Chicago, Detroit, Honolulu, Houston, Kansas City, Los Angeles, Miami, New Orleans, New York, Portland, Saipan, San Franciso, and Seattle.

Japan National Tourist Organization (JNTO)

WEB SITE
http://www.jnto.go.jp/

UNITED STATES
NEW YORK
One Rockefeller Plaza, Suite 1250
New York NY 10020

CHICAGO
401 N. Michigan Avenue, Suite 770
Chicago IL 60611

SAN FRANCISCO
360 Post Street, Suite 601
San Francisco CA 94108

LOS ANGELES
515 S. Figuera Street, Suite 1470
Los Angeles CA 90071

CANADA
TORONTO
165 University Avenue
Toronto, Ont. M5H 3B9

JAPAN
TOKYO
2-10-1 Yurakucho, Chiyoda-ku
Tokyo 100-0006

Goodwill Guides

Goodwill Guide volunteers are registered with the Japan National Tourist Organization and can be booked through any JNTO office.

Tourist Information Centers (TICs)

JNTO has Tourist Information Centers around the country that provide free travel information and literature on Japan. Staff members usually speak several languages and can make arrangements for home visits.

AIZU-WAKAMATSU
Aizu-Wakamatsu Station
   (0242)32-0688
Tsurugajo Castle Tourist Information
   (0242)29-1151

AOMORI
Aomori Prefectural TIC
   (0177)34-2500
Aomori Airport TIC
   (0177)39-4561

ARITA
JR Arita Station
   (0955)45-4052

ATAMI
Atami Station View Plaza
   (0557)81-6002

AWAJI
Awaji TIC
   (0799)72-0168

BEPPU
JR Beppu Station
   (0977)24-2838

CHIBA
Chiba City TIC
   (043)224-3939
Chiba Convention Bureau
   (043)296-0535

FUJIYOSHIDA
Fujiyoshida TIC
   (0555)22-7000

FUKUI
JR Fukui Station
   (0776)21-6492

FUKUOKA
Fukuoka City TIC
   (092)431-3003
Fukuoka International Association
   (092)733-2220
Fukuoka TIC
   (092)725-9100

FUKUYAMA
JR Fukuyama Station
   (0849)22-2869

HAKODATE
Hakodate TIC
   (0138)23-5440

HAKONE
Hakone Tourist Service
   (0460)5-8911

HIGASHINE (Yamagata Airport)
Yamagata Airport Information Center
   (0237)47-3111

HIKONE
JR Hikone Station
   (0749)22-2954

HIMEJI
JR Station Concourse
   (0792)85-3792

HIROSAKI
Hirosaki City Sightseeing.
(0172)37-5501
Hirosaki City Tourist Bureau
(0172)32-0524

HIROSHIMA
Hiroshima City Tourist Association
(082)247-6738

IMARI
Imari City Tourist Association
(0995)22-6920

ISE
Ise City Tourist Association
(0596)23-9655

ITO
Ito Station Travel Service
(0557)37-3291
Ito City Tourist Association
(0557)37-6105

KAGOSHIMA
Kagoshima City Tourist Service
(099)253-2500
Kagoshima Prefectural Tourist Center
(099)223-5771

KAMAKURA
Kamakura City Tourist Service
(0467)22-3350

KANAZAWA
Ishikawa Prefecture Kanazawa TIC
(0762)31-6311

KAWAGUCHIKO
Yamanashi Prefectural Fuji Center
(0555)72-0259
Kawaguichiko TIC
(0555)72-6700

KOBE
Kobe Information Center
(078)322-0220

KOCHI
JR Kochi Station
(0888)82-7777

KUMAMOTO
JR Kumamoto Station
(096)352-3743

KURASHIKI
JR Kurashiki Station (086)426-8681
Kurashiki-kan Information Center
(086)422-0542

KYOTO
Kyoto Main Office
(075)371-5649

MASHIKI
Kumamoto Airport Information Office
(096)232-2810

MATSUE
Matsue City Tourist Information
(0852)21-4034

MATSUMOTO
JR Matsumoto Station
(0263)32-2814

MATSUYAMA
Ehime Prefectural International Center
(089)943-6688
Matsuyama City Tourist Information
(089)931-3914

MIYAZAKI
JR Miyazaki Station
(0985)22-6469

MORIOKA
JR Morioka Station
(019)625-2090

NAGASAKI
Nagasaki City Tourist Association
(0958)23-3631
Nagasaki Prefectural Tourist Fed.
(0958)26-9407

NAGOYA
Chunichi Building TIC
(052)262-2918
Kanayama TIC
(052)323-0161
Nagoya International Center
(052)581-0100
Nagoya Port Visitor Information
Center
(052)654-7000
Nagoya Station TIC
(052)541-4301

NAHA
Okinawa Prefectural Tourist Fed.
(098)857-6884

NARA
Nara City Information Center
(0742)22-3900
Nara Prefectural TIC
(0742)23-8288
Nara Sarusawa Information
(0742)26-1991
Nara Tourist Information
(0742)24-4858

NARITA
Narita City TIC
(0476)24-3198
Narita Tourist Pavilion TIC
(0476)24-3232

NIIGATA
Niigata Station Bandaiguchi TIC
(025)241-7914

NIKKO
Nikko Information Center
(0288)53-3795
Tobu Nikko Station TIC
(0288)53-4511

OKAYAMA
Okayama City TIC
(086)222-2912
Okayama Prefectural International
Exchange Foundation
(086)256-2000

ONOMICHI
JR Shin-Onomichi
(0848)22-6900

OSAKA
JR Osaka Station Umeda
(06)6345-2189
JR Shin-Osaka Station
(06)6305-3311
Kansai International Airport
(0724)56-6025

OTSU
JR Otsu Station TIC
(077)522-3830

SAPPORO
Sapporo City Tourism Department
(011)211-2377
Sapporo Internat. Communications
(011)211-3678
Sapporo TIC
(011)232-7712

SENDAI
Sendai International Center
(022)265-2471
Sendai TIC, JR Sendai Station
(022)222-4069

SHIRAHAMA
Shirahama Station Tourist
Information.
(0739)42-2900

SHIZUOKA
Shizuoka City TIC
(054)252-4247

SUMOTO
Sumoto TIC
(0799)22-0742

TAKAMATSU
Takamatsu Tourist Information
(0878)51-2009

TAKARAZUKA
Takarazuka Tourist Information
(0797)81-5344

TAKAYAMA
Hida TIC JR Takayama Station
(0577)32-5328

TAKEO
JR Takeo Onsen Station
(0954)22-2542

TAZAWAKO
JR Tazawako Station
(0187)43-2111

TOKUSHIMA
Tokushima Prefecture, International
Exchange Association
(088)656-3303

TOKYO
Central Office
(03)3201-3331.
Narita International Airport
Terminal 2 (Main), Arrival Floor
(0476)34-6251
Terminal 1 (Branch), Arrival Floor
(0476)30-3383

TOYAMA
JR Toyama Station
(0764)32-9751

TSUCHIURA
Tsuchiura City TIC
(0298)21-4166

TSUKUBA
Tsukuba TIC
(0298)55-8155

URESHINO
Ureshino Onsen TIC
(0954)42-0336

UTSUNOMIYA
JR Utsunomiya Station
(028)636-2177

YAMAGATA
Yamagata Airport Information Center
(0237)47-3111
JR Yamagata Station
(0236)31-7865

YOKOHAMA
Convention & Visitors Bureau
(045)211-0111
Kanagawa Prefectural Tourist Assn.
(045)681-0007
Sanbo Center Office
(045)641-4759
JR Shin-Yokohama Station
(045)473-2895
Yokohama Station Information Center
(045)441-7300

Travel Companies

The following U.S. companies offer group tours to Japan led by English-speaking guides.

ABERCROMBIE AND KENT INTERNATIONAL
1520 Kensington Road,
Oak Brook IL 60521

ABSOLUTE ASIA
180 Varick Street
New York NY 10014

AMERICAN HOLIDAY TRAVEL
312 East First Street, Suite 341
Los Angeles CA 90012

AT LAST THE BEST! CUSTOM TRAVEL
10898 Dorchester Way,
Truckee CA 96161

CIRCA TOURS
1422 Euclid Avenue, Suite 1156
Cleveland OH 44115-2063

COSMOS
c/o Group Voyagers Inc.
5301 S. Federal Circle
Littleton CO 80123

EAST AND WEST TRAVEL CORP.
210 Post Street, Suite 810
San Francisco CA 94108

ESPRIT TRAVEL
2101 Wilshire Boulevard, Suite 101
Santa Monica CA 90403

FESTIVAL OF ASIA
400, Spear Street, #101
San Francisco CA 94105

FULTONEX
106 Fulton Street, 3rd floor
New York NY 10038

GEOGRAPHIC EXPEDITIONS
2627 Lombard Street,
San Francisco CA 94123

GLOBUS
c/o Group Voyagers Inc.,
5301 S. Federal Circle
Littleton CO 80123

GURNHAM GROUP
PO Drawer #6
Hilton Head SC 29938

**INTERNATIONAL HOLIDAY
TOUR & TRAVEL**
12792 Valley View, Suite C
Garden Grove CA 92845

JAPAN AND ORIENT
4025 Camino Del Rio South, Suite
3200
San Diego CA 92108

JOURNEYS EAST
PO Box 1161
Middletown CA 95461

JOURNEYS INTERNATIONAL
4011 Jackson Road
Ann Arbor MI 48103

**KINTETSU INTERNATIONAL
EXPRESS**
1325 Avenue of the Americas
New York NY 10019

KIRBY TOURS
2451 S. Telegraph
Dearborn MI 48124

**KOKUSAI INTERNATIONAL
TRAVEL**
4911 Warner Avenue, #221
Huntington Beach CA 92649

KOSAKURA TOURS & TRAVEL
350 Sansome Street, 10th floor,
San Francisco CA 94104

**NIPPON TRAVEL AGENCY
PACIFIC**
One Centerpointe Drive, Suite 400,
La Palma CA 90623

**NORTHWEST WORLD
VACATIONS/MLT
VACATIONS**
5130 County Road 101
Minnetonka MN 55345

ORIENT FLEXI-PAX TOURS
630 Third Avenue
New York NY 10017

PACIFIC DELIGHT TOURS
132 Madison Avenue
New York NY 10016

PACIFIC HOLIDAYS
2 West 45th Street, Suite 1102
New York NY 10036

**PACIFICO CREATIVE SERVICE
INC.**
700 S. Flower Street, Suite 1000,
Los Angeles CA 90017

PACIFIC PROTOUR
139 Kinderkamack Road,
Park Ridge NJ 07656

PANDA TRAVEL INC.
Panda Building, 2nd floor,
1017 Kapahulu Avenue
Honolulu HI 96816

PASSAGE TOURS
One Post Street, 7th floor,
San Francisco, CA 94104

SHOGUN TOURS
2115 Sawteller Boulevard,
Los Angeles CA 90025

TANAKA TRAVEL SERVICES
441 O'Farrell Street,
San Francisco CA 94102

TBI TOURS/GENERAL TOURS
53 Summer Street
Keene NH 03431

TRAVIS PACIFIC CORP.
1937 North Wilton Place,
Los Angeles CA 90068

UNITED VACATIONS
8907 N. Port Washington Road,
Milwaukee WI 53217

VISITS PLUS INC.
27 William Street, Suite 728,
New York NY 10005

WEST LA TRAVEL
12012 Ohio Avenue,
Los Angeles CA 90025

WILDERNESS TRAVEL
1102 Ninth Street,
Berkeley CA 94710

YAMATO TRAVEL
200 S. Pedro Street, Suite 502
Los Angeles CA 90012

INDEX